Secondary Behaviour Management
The Essentials

This concise book supplements the Routledge School Based Teacher Training Hub www.routledgeteachertraininghub.com

Chapters selected by Lizana Oberholzer, National Association of School Based Teacher Trainers and University of East London, UK.

Selected chapters from Routledge publications:

Geoff Barton, *Teach Now! The Essentials of Teaching: What You Need to Know to Be a Great Teacher* (ISBN 978-0-415-71491-4)

Philip Garner in Capel et al, *Learning to Teach in the Secondary School: A Companion to School Experience, 7th edition* (ISBN 978-1-138-78770-4)

Roland Chaplain, *Teaching Without Disruption in the Secondary School: A Practical Approach to Managing Pupil Behaviour* (ISBN 978-1-138-69069-1)

Simon Ellis and Janet Tod, *Promoting Behaviour For Learning in The Classroom: Effective Strategies, Personal Style and Professionalism* (ISBN 978-0-415-70449-6)

Terry Haydn, *Managing Pupil Behaviour: Improving the Classroom Atmosphere, 2nd edition* (ISBN 978-0-415-61432-0)

Alex Quigley, *The Confident Teacher: Developing Successful Habits of Mind, Body and Pedagogy* (ISBN 978-1-138-83234-3)

David Wright, *Classroom Karma: Positive Teaching, Positive Behaviour, Positive Learning* (ISBN 978-1-138-14337-1)

T0384737

Routledge
Taylor & Francis Group

LONDON AND NEW YORK

First published in 2020
by Routledge
2 Park Square, Milton Park, Abingdon, OX14 4RN

Routledge is an imprint of the Taylor & Francis Group, an informa business

Previously published as chapters in the following Routledge publications:
978-0-415-71491-4 *Teach Now! The Essentials of Teaching* (Chapters 15, 21, 24, 25),
978-1-138-78770-4 *Learning to Teach in the Secondary School* 7th edition (Unit 3.3),
978-1-138-69069-1 *Teaching Without Disruption in the Secondary School* (Chapter 1),
978-0-415-70449-6 *Promoting Behaviour For Learning in The Classroom*
(Chapter 6), 978-0-415-61432-0 *Managing Pupil Behaviour* 2nd edition (Chapter 4),
978-1-138-83234-3 *The Confident Teacher* (Chapter 9), 978-1-138-14337-1 *Classroom Karma* (Chapter 2).

British Library Cataloguing-in-Publication Data
A catalogue record for this book is available from the British Library

ISBN: 978-1-138-49134-2 (pbk)

Typeset in Times New Roman
by Integra Software Services Pvt. Ltd.

Contents

Introduction   vi

1 Using Teacher's Standard 7: How to Establish (and Maintain)
   Effective Classroom Discipline   1
   GEOFF BARTON

2 Using Teacher's Standard 1: How to Set High Expectations   6
   GEOFF BARTON

3 How to Use Language as a Teacher   10
   GEOFF BARTON

4 How to Use Classroom Routines to Establish Good Behaviour as the
   Norm   20
   GEOFF BARTON

5 Theory, Research and Behaviour Management   26
   ROLAND CHAPLAIN

6 Managing Student Behaviour   49
   ALEX QUIGLEY

7 Why do Some Children Behave and Some Do Not?   75
   DAVID WRIGHT

8 Managing Classroom Behaviour: Adopting a Positive Approach   98
   PHILIP GARNER

9 Effective Use of Positive Feedback and Rewards   118
   SIMON ELLIS AND JANET TOD

10 Managing Learning in Classrooms   131
   TERRY HAYDN

Introduction

Welcome to the Routledge Teacher Training Hub Series.

About the Hub

This concise book supplements the Routledge School Based Teacher Training Hub which you can find at www.routledgeteachertraininghub.com

The Hub has been developed in conjunction with teacher training experts and offers busy trainees and their mentors focussed, accessible, evidence-informed guidance that will help develop skills and confidence for successful classroom practice.

The chapters in this collection on the Hub explore one of the most challenging aspects of learning to teach in the secondary school: Managing behaviour. The Hub provides:

- Online access to ten chapters, carefully selected from across the breadth of Routledge's publishing, written by experts in the field, to cover core skills and knowledge for effective behaviour management.

- An introduction to each chapter, designed to show how the evidence applies to your setting and practice, and how you can build on the advice to develop and improve teaching.

- A self-audit test, to help you pinpoint gaps and understand where you will most benefit from skills and confidence development.

- Observation sheets, offering a framework that will help you focus and reflect when you're observing colleagues.

- Short mentor meeting guides to structure initial and ongoing meetings with your mentor, to help you get the most out of these important relationships.

21 Using Teachers' Standard 7

How to establish (and maintain) effective classroom discipline

This is the topic that worries would-be teachers more than any other. In fact, it worries all of us – the new kids on the block and the most seasoned of veterans. We'll mention it here, and then we'll come back to the topic later in this part of the book.

Teaching is unlike many other jobs, in that it isn't just something you do sitting at a desk or interacting with a team of colleagues. There is also this whole expectation that a group of up to thirty young people will be quiet and attentive in your presence. Whatever the stage we are at in our careers, we worry that sometimes they won't.

Managing good behaviour understandably forms one of the Teachers' Standards:

Teachers:

7(a) have clear rules and routines for behaviour in classrooms, and take responsibility for promoting good and courteous behaviour both in classrooms and around the school, in accordance with the school's behaviour policy;

7(b) have high expectations of behaviour, and establish a framework for discipline with a range of strategies, using praise, sanctions and rewards consistently and fairly;

7(c) manage classes effectively, using approaches which are appropriate to pupils' needs in order to involve and motivate them;

1

7(d) maintain good relationships with pupils, exercise appropriate authority, and act decisively when necessary.

So, how do we develop approaches and routines that are likely to lead to positive behaviour from students?

It can sometimes be counter-productive to watch really effective teachers at work. We can watch them with even the most challenging of groups and be drawn into the sense of mystery they exude.

When I was on teaching practice, many years ago, at a comprehensive school in Leicester, I watched my mentor, Bryan Palin, with a Year 8 group that had a pretty dodgy reputation.

At the end of the lesson, he needed them to be quiet, so that he could explain their homework. He stood and looked at them. He waited briefly. They fell silent. It was like watching a master conjuror at work, or a lion tamer.

He was doing something that looked so effortless and yet so unattainable that I almost felt like giving up on my chosen profession there and then.

So beware of watching charismatic teachers in full flow. Often, they will have been long established in the school, their reputations known by a previous generation of students and, in turn, by those students' parents.

Or it may be that they have roles in school that automatically bestow a kind of unspoken authority on them – as heads of year, for example, or similar roles that, in the eyes of the students, mean that these people wield intangible power.

No – far better to watch a teacher who uses techniques rather than the mysteries of personality to achieve high quality classroom discipline.

Fundamental to this will be 'withitness' – that sense of being attuned to the mood of the class, sensing when the pace is dropping, pre-empting a student who is drifting off task and about to do something foolish.

Withitness is, perhaps, our most important asset as teachers.

Teacher training

We learn it by spending time in lessons and getting a feel for how children behave. We learn it by knowing how to divert a student or a group from one task to another, how to increase pace and rejuvenate the energy of a classroom.

The insights into this comes from American researcher Jacob Kounin. Watching teachers working with challenging classes, he notes that the difference between effective and ineffective teachers is not how they stop bad behaviour at the end of an escalating chain of events, but whether they are 'able to stop the chain before it started'. You can read a brief account of his work in Malcolm Gladwell's enjoyable book of essays, *What the Dog Saw* (Allen Lane, 2009).

This means that setting the climate for learning, having routines, making explicit your expectations and then being highly attuned to the emotional temperature of your classroom – all of these matter hugely.

Reliance on complicated systems of sanctions *after* bad behaviour has happened will rarely be as effective as pre-empting it.

Here is how to set clear expectations. Think of it like this: We should aim to:

1   set out our expectations clearly;

2   model the behaviour and language we expect from students.

In responding to challenging behaviour, we should:

3   give students choices, rather than box them into a corner;

4   avoid public confrontation, where necessary by being prepared to defer issues to the end of a lesson.

In practice, this means that:

1   *As teacher, you create the climate for behaviour*: the way you greet students, where you stand to speak to them, the seating plan, the air temperature, the pace, the sense of structure and order . . . all of these are important.

3

2 *Emotional feedback is the most powerful type*: smiles, 'well done', thumbs up, using names. It may be backed up by, say, stickers, comments in the homework diary, postcards home and so on, but make sure you do the one-to-one stuff first.

3 *Courtesy isn't an optional extra*: expect and model good manners – remind students about saying 'please' and 'thank you', holding doors open, listening to others. Create an ethos that is high on expectations of courtesy by being hugely courteous yourself.

4 *Lesson planning shapes students' behaviour*: the biggest impact on the group's behaviour will be the work you expect them to do – clear, varied activities, good pace, appropriate challenge, a strong emphasis on what students are expected to learn.

5 *Deal with misbehaviour calmly*: focus on the effect of the poor behaviour on others; give a choice ('Are you going to sit and work there quietly, or do you need to move over here?'); move the student if necessary; but don't have a public confrontation – defer it to the end of the lesson, when other students have left.

That sense of calm, recognisable and familiar routines matters a lot in good teaching. It is part of the teacher's craft.

As you train to teach and as you establish yourself as a new teacher, build routines that you stick to and that your students expect from you – for example:

- where you stand as they arrive;
- what you ask them to do as they arrive (coats off, bags off desks, books, planners and pens on tables, and suchlike);
- how you take the register (explicitly, publicly and in complete silence);
- how you kick-start the lesson;
- how you signal that it's time for a transition between one activity and the next;

- how you pull activities together at the end of the lesson, reviewing learning, giving praise, packing the class up in good time.

Undertaking these approaches in a consistent way in every lesson won't make you robotic. Quite the reverse, in fact: they will help you to exude confidence, reassuring students that they know what to expect from you, and then – biggest secret of all – they will liberate you to be creative in the parts of teaching that really matter: the pedagogy, the stuff of your subject.

It is the biggest secret in teaching – that consistency liberates creativity.

So be consistent. Get the basics nailed. And then you can be creative within a clearly established framework.

TALKING POINTS

- Does anything here surprise you or seem unrealistic?
- What kinds of routine will you give special emphasis to in your teaching?

WHAT I LOVE ABOUT TEACHING

Spending time teaching a subject I really love. On a good day it feels a real privilege to do this. In teaching the subject and having to explain it, I find I have become much more of an expert.

15 Using Teachers' Standard 1

How to set high expectations

Standard 1 starts, quite rightly, with our expectations as teachers. Here's what it outlines:

> Set high expectations which inspire, motivate and challenge pupils

> 1(a) establish a safe and stimulating environment for pupils, rooted in mutual respect

> 1(b) set goals that stretch and challenge pupils of all backgrounds, abilities and dispositions

> 1(c) demonstrate consistently the positive attitudes, values and behaviour which are expected of pupils.

Note the emphasis on safety from the very beginning of the Standards. This isn't a reminder just for those who will be teaching in science laboratories, technology workshops and the like. It's for all teachers, of all subjects, in all classrooms and in other spaces around school.

Safety will include setting expectations about how students behave, how they relate to each other and how they use social media. It's a reminder of the responsibility we have as adults to all the young people in our care – the importance of setting clear boundaries and giving students a clear, if implicit, sense that they can trust us and that they are safe.

Expectations are the key to this, and often, in the best lessons, it means expecting more than the students might expect of themselves. That will include being intolerant of poor behaviour and sloppiness and lateness – but doing so in a way, as the Standards state, that demonstrates mutual respect.

This is an area that, for new teachers, can prove the hardest balance to strike, and it's one we will return to in our later discussions of classroom practice. 'Mutual respect' certainly doesn't mean chumminess – that is, perceiving the role of the teacher as being a surrogate friend to the students. It doesn't mean turning a blind eye to inappropriate behaviour or cultivating informality.

Mutual respect will most easily be demonstrated in the way you address students, the way you greet them at your classroom door, the way you avoid the 'dark sarcasm of the classroom', even when having to express exasperation with a student who is misbehaving.

How might you demonstrate that you are meeting the Standard?

You could make sure that, in every lesson plan, you make a note of health and safety issues – showing how you explicitly pre-empt risks. In some subjects, this will be more pressing than others. In Science, for example, having a note relating to equipment and goggles will demonstrate your pre-emptive thinking.

In other subjects, it may be that there is no obvious safety risk that seems to need mentioning on the lesson plan. In this case, you might simply have a space in your planning template that says 'special safety concerns', in which you write 'none'.

In other words, health and safety – your responsibility for the care of students – are so important that even writing 'none' signals a level of deliberately reflective practice. It shows that safety has been considered, that it matters.

Notice, however, that the Standard is about another aspect of our core business as teachers: the expectations we set of our students, irrespective of their backgrounds and personalities. With this Standard, of course you will want to *do* that, but you will also need to provide ongoing evidence.

Sometimes, as soon as we talk about making sure that we have high expectations and challenge students, it's easy to assume that this means challenging our most academically able students and diluting those expectations for those who find the work hard.

The real test for us as teachers is to set work that is appropriately challenging for *all* our students.

It may be that your school has a house style on lesson objectives. Some expect a kind of three-level set of targets – what everyone in the group must achieve, what most might achieve and what some could achieve. These can feel a bit contrived.

Nevertheless, after establishing good behaviour, perhaps the most demanding part of a teacher's job is teaching in a way that challenges the range of students in a class. That doesn't mean – as we were once madly instructed – having an individual objective for each child. That would be impossible in most groups. It does mean demonstrating what you will do – and then have done – so that your ablest students feel challenged in a lesson and across a term, and the same for middle- and lower-ability students.

The longer you teach, the more intuitive this becomes.

You get to know more specifically what you might expect of students working at different levels of skill and knowledge. This, in turn, helps you to give them better quality feedback and, in due course, to be able to make suggestions to them as you move about the class about how they might improve their work.

But at this stage, you need to provide evidence that you are setting high expectations. Here's how to do this:

Make sure your lesson planning includes objectives or targets or a summary of knowledge and skills to be learned that are challenging. You might label them as such to make explicit that you are setting stretching tasks for students.

In your marking and feedback, mention from time to time where a student has responded at a high level to a challenging target.

Comment on how he or she has risen to the challenge and say 'well done'. Then, keep a copy of some examples of your marking in your portfolio (a single example won't be as persuasive as three to five examples from different groups).

Periodically – perhaps once each half-term – take a copy of a student response that exemplifies the high standards you have set. This won't only be in the content of the work that has been produced; it will show up in the presentation too. High expectations mean being persistent about how work should look – demanding high quality accuracy and clarity. This is particularly important from students whose backgrounds may not reinforce the high expectations you set.

Therefore, from time to time, take a copy as evidence of the high expectations you have of all your students. Keep it in a sub-section of your portfolio and label it something like 'Challenging Expectations'.

Finally, remember that any supportive comments students make about how you help them to improve their work – for example, in their written response to your marking, or in occasional emails or cards from them or their parents – are also important, objective sources of evidence for the high expectations you set.

It will seem, to some of us, a bit odd, even a bit cynical, to be saving these in a portfolio of evidence, but that is what we should do, because meeting the Teachers' Standards is something that needs to be built on a range of evidence rather than hearsay or reported good intentions.

TALKING POINTS

- What is your own experience of expectations – of parents and teachers who expected a lot from you, or expected too little?
- How would you characterise your own expectations of what all your students might achieve?

24 How to use language as a teacher

This title isn't necessarily as daft as it seems.

Language is a teacher's bread and butter. It is what we use. Watch a great teacher of Mathematics at work and what you'll see is the clever use of explanation, of questioning, of not always giving an answer, of pausing, using silence, lifting an eyebrow.

Skilfully using language – spoken language and body language – is fundamental to becoming a great teacher. That's why it deserves more attention from the very start of our careers, from our earliest training onwards.

Partly that's because it is during our earliest time as teachers that bad habits can set in. Unless we have someone critiquing our work periodically, or put ourselves through the self-conscious process of recording and listening back to ourselves, then it is easy for certain mannerisms, certain words and phrases, to lodge themselves in our way of speaking.

That is why, right at the start of becoming a teacher, it is worth looking at how to talk as a teacher – that is, how to use language effectively.

Insist on silence

One of the main differences between a lesson taught by an expert teacher and one taught by a newcomer is that the expert will insist on – absolutely demand – silence when he or she is speaking.

Teacher training

This arises from a kind of inner confidence, a self-belief that is – of course – a bit of a con-trick. It is built on the assumption that when I, as the main adult in the classroom, speak, then you, the class of students, must listen.

Without this unwritten agreement between teacher and students, high-quality learning is very unlikely to happen. So, from the very start, insist on silence. Many of us do this by having a trigger phrase or two, essentially saying to students, 'Listen to me'.

What you don't want to do is to raise your voice to gain the attention of the class. There is little that is more unbecoming, and sometimes painfully humiliating to witness, than a fledgling or veteran teacher who is working harder and harder in beseeching the class to be quiet.

That is why many of us use phrases such as, 'Thank you. Pens down and everyone looking this way'.

There are a couple of points to note here. First, 'thank you' is a more powerful than 'please'. It is built on the assumption that you will do what I say, rather than require me to plead with you. Make 'thank you' part of your verbal repertoire.

Note also the physical expectation of stillness that is required in the 'pens down' command. We know that there is no logical reason that students cannot hold a pen and listen perfectly well, but the phrase requires them to do something and then gives you, as teacher, a clear visual clue about who is listening.

If you are softly spoken, you might clap your hands to gain attention as you say the phrase. I sometimes tap some keys or a board rubber on the desk. I have – as I'm recommending you should have – some familiar and repeatable cues to students that it is time for them to be still and listen in silence.

Then, you need to insist on it, so if someone at the side of the room hasn't put her pen down, look at her until she does, or say 'Pen down, please' or – raising the stakes slightly with a question – 'Did you hear me ask for pens down and looking this way?'

You will want to develop your own verbal and visual cues. They will be an essential part of the process of developing your air of authority in the classroom, making it easier to draw the class back to full attention, to explain things, to move the lesson on. So be ruthless on this one: insist on silence.

Ask better questions

Teachers ask a lot of questions, usually requiring answers that we already know ourselves. It is one of the more surreal aspects of how teachers use language – unlike in the real world out there, our questions aren't usually designed to find out things that we don't know; they're to find out whether our students know what we know.

High quality questions are an important feature of high quality teaching. That means thinking about the purpose of the questions you ask, thinking whether there might be other ways of getting a wider range of students in the class to demonstrate their knowledge, rather than the one who directly answers your question.

I suggest the following elements will improve your questioning skills.

First, create a culture in which questions aren't just the age-old ritual of a teacher asking something, a few familiar hands going up, and the same student enthusiasts dutifully parroting their answer, while the rest of the class listens passively, or doesn't.

A culture for better questioning will arise if you can do two things.

First, try to break the tyranny of students putting their hands up. Develop a sense that anyone in the room can be asked to give an answer, that there's no need to put up a hand. This often sounds counter-intuitive to teachers who haven't seen it in action, and it can be perceived as unnerving for students, who may not know what to say and, therefore, leave embarrassing, unwanted silences.

That is why, second, together with the no-hands-up approach, you must build in student thinking time, or 'oral rehearsal'. Thinking time means saying to students:

Teacher training

> I'm going to ask some people to explain to me why earthquakes happen. I'm looking for two or three main reasons based on what we've been studying. Have one minute to think what you're going to say and then I'll choose some people.

Oral rehearsal means giving students that minute or so – no more – to rehearse their answer with a partner. This builds their confidence, gets over some self-consciousness issues and can lead to better-expressed answers.

These two approaches will begin to create a culture in which all students know that your questions are designed for all to answer, rather than just the keenies.

That is where you need to ask better questions. These will more often than not be 'how?' and 'why?' questions, rather than 'what?'.

'What?' questions are fine for recalling basic knowledge, for checking students know facts and theories, but it is the 'how?' and 'why?' questions that take them deeper, that lead to exploration of processes, that lead us further into students having the skills to apply, analyse, synthesise and evaluate.

That is where, from the outset, we should plan our questions: if we are clear about what skills and knowledge we want our students to demonstrate, then we will get better, deeper answers from better questioning, probably through fewer questions than the old scattergun approach led to, supported by a culture of no hands up, thinking time and oral rehearsal.

One other thing: don't accept the first good answer you get from a student. In fact, try to comment less on answers than teachers traditionally have. It is all too easy for us to ask a question, choose someone with their hand up, listen to their answer, say 'good answer' and then move on.

If one student is answering a question, we can't know whether other students are also understanding to the same degree.

So develop a repertoire in response to students' answers. Rather than accept the first response you get, make it part of the Q&A culture of your classroom that students know that you are likely to ask someone else for their answer, and then someone else; and then to ask someone else to comment on which of the three answers so far he most agrees with and why; and then to do the same with another student.

Thus, questioning becomes a core activity in which we work as a group to explore issues, to deepen our collective understanding, to make judgements about what has been said and to explore how we might express our learning better.

Questioning in this way is perhaps the most important skill we have as teachers – it is a type of human interaction that other forms of learning (e.g. on line) seem unlikely to replicate. So use every opportunity to develop your questioning skills and, when possible, get to watch other teachers – good or bad – at work.

All of it will help you, through practice and reflection, to become a better questioner and, what follows from it, a better teacher.

Explain more effectively

This is an underrated part of what we have to do as teachers. We have to explain stuff. Whether it is giving an account of something in our subject – 'here's why the Periodic Table matters' – or describing how today's lesson will unfold, we spend a lot of time explaining.

Experience suggests that clear, understandable explanations are essential. Too often, what students complain of is teachers who talk too much or repeat too much or go into too much detail.

Learning to explain with clarity and flair is essential. It is also the way that you will show students how to use vocabulary that is essential for their subject. You will show them how to speak like a scientist, historian or musician. It is one of the most important responsibilities you have.

Here is how to do it. First, know what you want to say. Give students the outline, but, if there is additional detail, you might have that on the whiteboard and simply refer them to it. There are times when it is quite right that you should talk a lot, especially as the expert in the room.

Teacher training

However, explanations usually benefit from being concise and providing an overarching, understandable shape to what students need to take in.

That's where being redundant rather than repetitive in your speech makes a difference. Redundancy is a term from linguistics and (in this case) from rhetoric. Here is how a Wikipedia entry explains it (perfectly): 'Through the use of repetition of certain concepts, redundancy increases the odds of predictability of a message's meaning and understanding to others'.

That is precisely what I am recommending – that you deploy key words and phrases redundantly to add clarity to your explanations and instructions. That is not the same as repeating information that you have already mentioned.

So an explanation about how students are expected to approach a task might sound like this:

> We've been studying Elizabethan England for a few lessons now. Today it's time for you to demonstrate to me what you have learned. You're going to do this in three ways.
>
> First, you're going to work in a three to decide what the key ideas of the period are. You'll present these on a one-screen poster or PowerPoint page.
>
> Second, you'll think about how to present this knowledge to the rest of the group in a two-minute 'speed dating' exercise. There are more details about what's required in this second task here on the board.
>
> Finally, you'll be visiting each other group and absorbing their information as quickly as possible, ready to demonstrate to me in the last twenty minutes that you have become experts in this period.
>
> So there are three main tasks you'll need to do, and just forty minutes to work through them.

As ever, an outline of teacher speech like this feels phoney when written out on the page. Let's accept that. But it does illustrate the way in which connectives ('first, second, finally') are being used to help structure the explanation in students' minds. It uses words such as 'this' and 'here' to draw attention to additional information. It uses the classic 'rule of three' to organise the sequence of activities and bring clarity.

There is one other essential ingredient in effective explanations: using metaphor. Great teachers can take complex subjects and render them simple, but not too simple. They can help students to understand processes that initially baffle them.

Metaphor is when we compare one thing with another. We get students to visualise something abstract or unseen (molecules) and use language that helps them to visualise what might be happening ('dancing', 'bumping into each other', 'bouncing faster and faster').

It is worth watching some great teachers at work in, say, Physics or Chemistry or History, watching the way they are able to help their students to absorb the essential essence of concepts and processes by their ability to make analogies and tell stories. Being able to do so will make your own explanations clearer and more powerful.

Read aloud well

There will be times when you need to read aloud from a textbook or handout or article. Do this well. Model to students what good reading aloud sounds like and how we use the structure and punctuation in texts to help us understand them.

Here are some hints:

- Don't get students reading a text aloud unless you have given them preparation time: it can undermine their confidence in reading publicly. Instead, you read.

- Make sure you have read the text through in advance, so that you are familiar with it: this will save you getting tangled on any parts that are obscurely expressed or badly phrased.

Teacher training

- Use the punctuation to guide your reading: pause at commas and full stops for slightly longer than you might expect to. Overall, read a bit more slowly than feels natural.

- Insist that students follow the text as you read – have it on a screen at the front of the room, or in front of each one. In this way, they get to see how confident readers (that is, you!) read texts, how we use intonation, and how we use punctuation to demarcate units of meaning.

- Seize any opportunity you can to make explicit to students how you read, decode and interpret a text – like this:

Before reading:

> So before I read the text I look at the title. I make a prediction about what the article might be about. I also try to work out how reliable this text will be – is it by an author I know of? Is it in a publication that's trustworthy? How can I tell? Knowing these things will help me as I read to know whether to trust exactly what is being said, or whether I should be more cautious about it.

During reading:

> I've paused at this word because it's one that I don't know – or at least I'm not confident that I know it. So I'm wondering which words it reminds me of – are there words with a similar start ('photo-')? Can I use them to help me to work out what the meaning of this word is? Does the context (plants and light) help? Has the writer included a glossary at the end of the article that I can refer to, or does the next sentence help me to work out the meaning more clearly?

After reading:

> So, I think a bit about what the article is saying. I try to sum up its main points. I could do this in three or four bullet

points, or in a spider diagram. What I'm trying to do is to make sure that I have fully grasped what the writer has said.

My next job is to think about how he has said it. That's going to let me move on to higher skills – deciding whether I agree with the writer, whether this is a text I should trust or dispute.

In reading aloud well, and in commenting on what you do before, during and after reading, you perform one of the most important acts a teacher can do – initiating those students for whom reading is often an alien, unfathomable process and bringing them into the domain of the literate. You help them, in other words, to see why the ability to read well is so central to being able to learn well. You demystify the mysterious.

Don't underestimate language

If you have read the preceding advice and thought anything from 'not relevant to me' to 'he's a literacy nutter', stop now. Language is how we communicate. It is how we understand one another. In schools and colleges, it is how we pass on knowledge and skills from one generation to the next. It is how we help students to understand ideas, to develop their intellect, to build their social skills, to refine how to be human.

Language is what defines us. So don't underestimate its importance in class.

Experience tells me that, if a teacher of Mathematics or Design Technology or Science or English isn't much good, language is often near the heart of the issue.

Whether it is that we are not explaining well enough, or asking too many questions, or simply talking too much – language can have a huge effect on reducing our power as teachers.

So make it an ongoing priority to think about language, to use it well and to monitor what you are doing with it.

In particular, be attuned to the dreadful, irksome language traits that we can all pick up. These are the mannerisms that we notice

Teacher training

in other staff when they lead assemblies, or we hear in colleagues at staff meetings, or in students when they speak in class.

They are the fillers and the repetitions and the clichés – the 'likes', the 'okays' the 'you know what I means'.

Just as we need, from time to time, to purge our hard drives and reboot our servers, so we need to be mindful of our own speech habits. Irritating and unnecessary verbal mannerisms can set in and, if we don't notice them ourselves, they can harden and fester.

So, as the final message of this chapter, regularly pay attention to the way you use language – whether it involves you asking a colleague to observe you and give feedback, or (wincingly) recording your own lesson on video or audio, or using student evaluation that asks for open feedback on your teaching style.

All of this will make you a much better teacher.

TALKING POINTS

- Which aspects of this unit do you need to think more about?
- Which other teachers have you observed and admired or winced at?
- What verbal mannerisms are you already conscious of developing?

25 How to use classroom routines to establish good behaviour as the norm

Creating and maintaining a calm, orderly ethos is important. Effective learning can rarely take place without it.

It is easy to overcomplicate the management of behaviour using systems designed to reward students' good behaviour, to deter them from behaving badly and to punish them if they transgress.

All schools are likely to have something at the heart of their ethos that is designed to do this. At the very least, the school will want to encourage students to do things that are nice rather than nasty.

However, especially as new teachers, we can become fixated on these systems, thinking that they are the key to good behaviour.

In reality, students will behave well because they see the relevance of what they are doing, or because they like it, or because some other, intangible reward for doing it motivates them.

That is where classroom routines are important in setting the tone for behaviour, in establishing a culture from which positive, courteous behaviour arises, almost unthinkingly.

Here are some ground rules.

In general, as stated earlier, we should aim to:

- set out our expectations clearly;
- model the behaviour and language we expect from students.

Teacher training

For the majority of our students, for most of the time, this approach, consistently applied, will suffice. Good behaviour from most members of our classes will follow.

If, however, you have to respond to poor behaviour, you should:

- Give students choices, rather than box them into a corner.
- Avoid public confrontation, where necessary, by being prepared to defer issues to the end of a lesson.

Setting the tone for behaviour means using a series of routines and sticking to these every lesson. Here is what I would recommend:

At the start of lessons:

- Try to be in the room before students arrive, standing at the door as they come in.
- Ensure that coats have been taken off, books and equipment are quickly taken out, and bags are placed on the floor; planners or homework diaries should be on students' desks.
- Aim to take a register within the first ten minutes of the lesson (even if not formally, by calling out names, it is important that students *know* that the register is nevertheless being taken).
- Make the learning objectives clear, and return to them at the end of the lesson.

When dealing with lateness:

- Never ignore lateness. You mustn't be seen to condone it. Politely ask any late students why they are late, and then decide quickly whether this is an acceptable explanation. (One acceptable reason for several students arriving late might, for example, be that this morning's assembly overran.) If there isn't an acceptable reason, don't provoke a public row: simply say that you will want to see the late students at the end of the lesson when the others leave. Then, for a first offence, make a point of writing (slowly) in the student's planner that he or she arrived late. This means that the parent and tutor should see the note. You, meanwhile, have inconvenienced the student by keeping him or her back to make the note and signalled to other, prompt, students that you won't turn a blind eye to lateness.

Using praise:

- Aim to praise students as much as possible, but make it meaningful praise – that is, commenting on things that matter.
- Praise might include: saying 'well done', issuing a merit sticker or some other device advocated in the school's behaviour code or making a note in the planner.
- Of all of these, saying 'well done' (or words to that effect) is probably the most important.

Dealing with disruption:

- Make it clear to a misbehaving student how this is affecting the class (that is, focus on the misdemeanour, not the person).
- Ask the student whether she would prefer to move to sit nearer to you rather than stay where she currently is.
- If necessary, move the student.
- If behaviour problems persist, defer the matter to the end of the lesson and deal with the issue in private. Unless it is very significant, you are far better tackling such concerns without an audience of curious students.

Finishing lessons:

- Build in time for students to review what they have learned, referring back to the learning objectives; write homework on the board and ensure that it is copied into the planner; check that students have done this by walking around the room, looking at planners.

Teacher training

- Expect students to pack away quietly, tidying the furniture (chairs on desks at the end of the day) and picking up any residual litter; leave the board clean.

- Dismiss the quietest row/groups first (rather than all at once, or by gender), preferably standing at the door as they leave.

  Establish classroom routines:

- Arrive at the room before students arrive and get the register ready; stand at the door as the students come in.

- Leave the door to the classroom open for five minutes; any students arriving after this time are officially late and should hand you their planner; see these students at the end of the lesson, having made a note in the 'comments' section that they were late to your lesson; their tutor and parents will then become aware; also record the late and any comments on the register.

- Consciously decide upon and plan the seating arrangements for students, rather than leaving them to decide where they wish to sit; make it clear every lesson that the decision about where students sit is yours; help yourself by moving students around frequently; keep reinforcing the fact that this is your territory.

- Ensure that coats have been taken off, books and equipment are quickly taken out, and bags are placed on the floor; planners should be on students' desks.

- Take a register within the first few minutes of the lesson; do this publicly – for example, by calling students names out while they sit in silence; this reinforces their awareness that attendance is being checked.

- Make the learning objectives clear – or whatever formulation you use of what students will learn this lesson – usually by having them on display, and return to them at the end of the lesson.

- Aim to praise students as much as possible, formally and informally.

- Give thinking time after asking a question (e.g. 'Have five seconds to think what your answer is'); this will lead to far better answers.

- Ask fewer questions, using more open-ended styles of question ('Explain to me *how/why* this happens . . .'; 'What are the three main ingredients in this process . . .?'; 'How do we know what the author thinks . . .?').

- Limit the use of putting hands up (whereby the same small number of students often answer most of the questions); instead, say, 'Discuss what your answer will be for thirty seconds, then I'll ask people to tell me – no need to put hands up'.

- Promote active student participation in learning, with them leading starters and plenaries, chairing meetings, giving feedback on each other's performances, and so on.

- Make it clear to a misbehaving student how this is affecting the class (focusing on the misdemeanour, not the person).

When a student is disrupting or disturbing others, you might:

- stop teaching and wait for them to calm down;

- have a quiet word about the need to behave;

- ask them to stop the disruption;

- move them to a different seat;

- in exceptional circumstances (such as serious defiance), call for support from another member of staff.

Teacher training

TALKING POINTS

- There is a lot here to assimilate: which parts do you most agree with? Which are you less certain of?
- What kinds of routine will become part of your repertoire to give students a consistent set of expectations of your teaching?

Chapter 1

Theory, research and behaviour management

Rigorously researching what works best in respect of managing pupil behaviour should be routine in education. Judging the validity of a claim that one approach is better than another should be based on objective empirical research, not what sounds like a good idea. Unfortunately, that is not always the case in reality. Many books on managing behaviour often contain statements like 'this book avoids dry/boring/complex theory and research' and go on to say that the book is based on common sense and on the author's experience as a teacher. Out-of-hand rejection of theory and research in this way demonstrates ignorance of what a theory is. These authors' collections of anecdotes, good ideas and tips collectively constitute their *implicit theory* of how to manage behaviour in class. As discussed in Chapter 3, we all have our own implicit theories about a range of phenomena, including intelligence (Blackwell *et al.*, 2007) and personality (Baudson and Preckel, 2013), and we all have theories about behaviour (Geeraert and Yzerbyt, 2007).

'Practical people' often believe that 'the facts' (i.e. their experience) speak for themselves – but they don't. Facts are interpreted, and the interpretation relies on implicit theories that go beyond the facts to give them meaning. Despite their limitations, personal theories might work satisfactorily for some people most of the time, but those theories may prove wrong, inappropriate or disastrous for someone else. Should the 'tip' you are given not work for you, what do you conclude and what do you do next? Picking up ideas as you go along may work for gardening, but I consider teaching to be a profession, and being professional should include having the particular knowledge and skills necessary to do your job. Just because behaviour management training has had a low profile in teacher education should not mean that the research evidence available about what works best should be ignored.

The term 'evidence-based practice', increasingly used in education, means adopting methods based on sound theoretical principles and supported by empirical research. It applies to all areas of pedagogy, including behaviour management as the DfE recommendations for behaviour management training made clear:

> Theoretical knowledge: trainees should know about scientific research and developments, and how these can be applied to understanding, managing and changing children's behaviour.
>
> (DfE, 2012)

Whilst there are a number of established theories, models and frameworks available with contrasting views on how to manage behaviour, I have chosen to focus on those supported by the strongest empirical evidence. If you wish to know more about other models, Porter (2006) provides a useful overview of seven contrasting approaches.

The cognitive-behavioural approaches, models and methods that follow are housed in empirical evidence drawn from educational, psychological and neuroscientific research about behaviour management and wider aspects of human behaviour. Applied correctly, they will provide you with a framework on which to organise your classroom management planning to quickly establish and maintain your authority as a teacher, develop pupils' engagement with learning, build effective classroom relationships, create the conditions for teaching and learning and help develop pupils' self-control and social competence.

Behavioural approaches focus solely on observable behaviour, whereas cognitive-behavioural approaches focus on both observable (overt behaviour) and thinking and emotions (covert behaviour). Behavioural approaches change behaviour by reinforcement and/or punishment. Cognitive approaches change the behaviour by changing the thinking (and emotions) behind the behaviour, actively trying to persuade people to think differently. It follows that cognitive-behavioural approaches (CBA) combine the two in different proportions, depending on the specific approach. CBA have been shown to be effective in decreasing disruptive behaviour in the classroom (Sukhodolsky and Scahill, 2012); to improve pupils' self-control (Feindler *et al.*, 1986) and to have lasting effects (Lochman, 1992).

The following descriptions of the theories and models have been simplified to make them more accessible and usable in the classroom. Numerous references are included throughout the chapter for anyone wishing to develop an in-depth knowledge.

Behavioural approaches (BA)

The basic premise of these approaches is that all behaviour, including unacceptable behaviour, is learned through reinforcement and deterred by punishment. Elements of BA are evident in all schools, where pupils receive rewards (e.g. praise, tokens, or having tea with the head, etc.) for behaving as required or sanctions (e.g. detention) for misbehaving. Unfortunately, in many instances, because the principles underpinning the approach are misunderstood, they are ineffective, or their effectiveness is limited.

BA offer a scientific approach to behaviour management, since they are based on structured observation, manipulating the environment and measurement of behaviour. There are three areas of focus: what occurs before a behaviour (antecedent) or what starts it off; the behaviour itself; and what follows or keeps it going (consequence), from which a hypothesis is created and tested (see Figure 1.1). For example, Miss Jones has difficulty getting pupils to stop talking so that she can give out instructions. She decides to introduce an incentive for speeding up responses to her request for pupils to stop talking and face her when she claps her hands. She claps her hands (antecedent) and the first five pupils who stop talking immediately (behaviour) receive a sticker (consequence). She repeats this process until satisfied that the routine is established. The objective being for the class to complete the task competently and quickly.

Whilst behaviourists recognise that something goes on inside the brain (covert behaviour), they argue that we can only theorise about *what* the

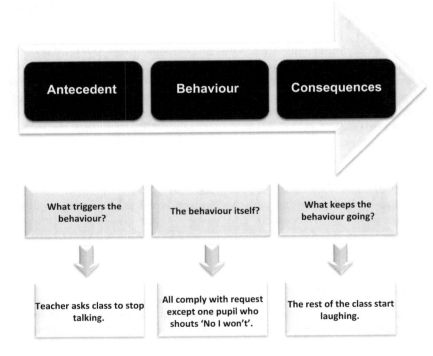

Figure 1.1 ABC model of behaviour.

individual is thinking and how their previous history *might* have influenced that behaviour. This focus on the measurement of overt behaviour is not limited to behaviourists. Other approaches in psychological and educational research also rely on measuring behaviour to support their theories. Cognitive psychologists might compare time taken to complete a maths task and infer how different metacognitive strategies are advantageous or disadvantageous in problem-solving. Neuroscientists measure performance on a task whilst mapping brain activity using scanning equipment, inferring which brain regions might be associated with specific behaviour.

Neuroscience has provided information about the effect of rewards, punishment and motivation on brain activity, elements central to the behavioural approach. For example, dopamine, a neurotransmitter, helps control the brain's reward and pleasure centres, notably through pathways between the limbic system and the forebrain (Thompson, 2000). It also enables individuals to prioritise rewards and to take action to approach them. At the very moment your brain recognizes something it likes (e.g. food), it will make you *think* it is good and will encode that information and remember that you liked it (Galván, 2013). Research has also demonstrated that the substantial behavioural changes during adolescence are largely believed to be driven by rewards, including monetary, novel and social rewards, and by extension, the reward-sensitive dopamine system (Galván *et al.*, 2006; Van Leijenhorst *et al.*, 2010). This helps explain why, if a teacher picks the right reward and correct rate of rewarding, he/she is able to manipulate behaviour and engagement with learning since it is associated with pleasure and reward. A reward does not need to be present to have an effect, as dopamine can be released in anticipation or triggered by association with a stimulus, e.g. a teacher opening a drawer that contains *desirable* stickers, which are associated with a particular behaviour.

Competent teachers can make managing pupils (including those others find difficult) look comparatively easy. Teacher A walks into a room and gives a disappointed look at those pupils who are misbehaving, and those pupils all stop talking, sit down and face the front. New teacher B repeats the same behaviour, but the noise continues – begging the question why? There may be a number of possible explanations, one being a lack of association between stimulus (teacher B's expression) and the required response and/or the consequences of not doing so – an association that needs to be established and reinforced over time to become automatic.

The two most familiar origins of behavioural approaches are classical and operant conditioning.

Classical conditioning

Classical conditioning is the most basic form of associative or automatic learning in which one stimulus brings about a response.

The Nobel Prize winner Ivan Pavlov, known for his research with dogs (and children), is less well-known as being one of the most influential neurophysiologists of his century (Pickehain, 1999). Pavlov believed dogs were hard-wired to salivate in response to food (a natural response), but he trained them to salivate at the sound of a bell (an unnatural response). He noticed that the dogs in the laboratory would begin to salivate in anticipation of food, for example, when an assistant entered the laboratory at feeding time or when they heard the 'click' made by the machine that distributed the food – both unnatural responses. So he began ringing a bell at the same time he provided the food to teach an association between the unnatural and natural stimulus. Initially, the bell was a neutral stimulus, i.e. it did not produce a salivary response. However, after repeated pairings between bell and food, the bell in the absence of food provided the trigger for the dogs to salivate. This relationship is known as contiguity – an association between two events that occur closely together in time. Association learning can be observed in all classrooms. Pupils learning to respond in a particular way to unnatural stimuli, e.g. lining up when a bell is rung.

Humans have a distinct advantage over dogs – that is, language, which means that the desired behaviour can initially be stated explicitly – e.g. stand up, sit down, stop talking, or line up – then replaced with more subtle nonverbal triggers such as gestures (e.g. the teacher claps or raises their hand) to initiate the required behaviour (see Table 1.1).

Competent teachers spend the first couple of weeks with a new class establishing routines and teaching their pupils to associate particular cues with specific behavioural requirements in their classrooms (Leinhardt *et al.*, 1987). Trainee teachers taking over classes in which routines are established and efficient can find it daunting, especially if the pupils do not respond to their signals in the same way as they do for the regular teacher. It is essential, therefore, to understand how such behaviours are established and how to develop these routines quickly in order to help a novice teacher feel in control.

Table 1.1 Using classical conditioning to establish a basic routine behaviour

Stage	Teacher behaviour	Pupil behaviour
Stage 1 No routine in place	Claps Tells pupils to face her	➡ Pupils don't face her ➡ Pupils face her
Stage 2 Establishing routine	Tells pupils to face her whilst clapping	➡ Pupils face her
Stage 3 Routine established	Claps	➡ Pupils face her

Operant conditioning

The second approach is operant conditioning (OC). The basic premise of OC is that any behaviour that is followed by reinforcement is likely to be repeated. If a pupil blows a raspberry and the class laughs, she is likely to do so again – laughter being the reinforcer. In contrast, behaviour followed by punishment is less likely to be repeated. OC owes much to the work of B.F. Skinner (1974) who explained learning in terms of the relationship between stimulus, response and reinforcement. For Skinner, a stimulus or response should be defined by *what it does*, rather than how it looks or what it costs; in other words, a functional definition of behaviour. Definitions need not be fixed in advance; a definition can be selected according to what works (Skinner, 1961). OC is a pragmatic approach to specifying behaviour based on a functional definition, meaning that activities should be designed to produce orderly results. For Skinner, the emphasis should always be on *positive reinforcement of required behaviour* rather than on punishment of undesirable behaviour.

Operant conditioning is used in all schools. For example, verbally supporting a pupil (consequence) for completing a task (behaviour) when asked (stimulus) *may* increase the likelihood that he/she will continue to make an effort, in order to gain more verbal support. However, this depends on the degree to which a pupil values that consequence. Being praised publicly may not be seen as rewarding by some pupils, who would rather just have a quiet word or a thumbs up from that teacher (Burnett, 2001). Other pupils will not respond to verbal support but will respond to tangible rewards, e.g. stickers. Other pupils are self-reinforcing, in effect they reward themselves for their successes – i.e. they complete tasks because they enjoy it. Put simply, any behaviour that is followed by *something* that an individual finds pleasurable, is likely to be repeated and becomes learned. *Anything* that follows a behaviour to keep it going or strengthens it is termed a 'reinforcer'.

Difficulties in school often result from pupils being inappropriately reinforced for unacceptable behaviour – an action known as negative reinforcement (not to be confused with punishment). The following case study illustrates negative reinforcement.

Case study

From Year 7, Craig had never enjoyed English nor had he experienced much success in the subject. Now in Year 9, he would often not pay attention to Mr Smith, his English teacher, and would frequently disturb other pupils. When Craig's disruptive behaviour became unacceptable to Mr Smith, he would send him to Mrs Wills, the head of year, where he would stay until the end of the English lesson. As Mrs Wills was invariably

> busy, she would give Craig jobs, such as tidying an equipment cupboard or sorting papers, which Craig did enthusiastically. These behaviours – misbehaving in English class and getting sent to the head of year – became ritualised behaviour for all involved and proved hard to break.

There are four points I would make about this case study. First, it is not acceptable for a pupil to be spending time off legitimate learning tasks (however important the equipment cupboard might be). Second, the reinforcer in this case (tidying the store cupboard) was preferable to having to spend time learning English, despite teachers informing Craig of the importance of English to his future. It is a reinforcer because it is perpetuating the undesirable behaviour. Third, the ritual provided a coping strategy for all three individuals. Fourth, the habitual nature of the process made it difficult for people to stand back and think out alternative ways of dealing with the problem, so they had become locked into a negative cycle.

Negative cycles can become automatic, destructive and accepted as 'normal' behaviour. Many such cycles occur initially by chance and often none of the parties involved are aware of its development. A class observing a negative cycle developing between a teacher and a pupil frequently collude to focus attention away from their own misbehaviour. Pupils regularly in trouble are often automatically blamed, sometimes even in their absence. Making a conscious effort to change what has become a negative ritual can have significant effects. Being more polite when you think the group is rude and ignorant, or using humour when you would routinely use a reprimand can produce positive effects. Changing the ritual is, in effect, changing the link between stimulus, response and reinforcer.

Rewards and reinforcement

Rewards and sanctions are referred to in school behaviour policies and in government publications (e.g. DfE, 2014a) and, as such, they represent a loose connection to behavioural approaches – loose because behaviourists distinguish between the terms 'reward' and 'reinforcement'. Rewards vary between both schools and classrooms. A reward (e.g. certificates, house points, special activities) is something that is given to someone to denote an accomplishment. On the other hand, reinforcement is an effect, which must lead to an increase in a specific behaviour (Maag, 2001) and not all 'rewards' do. A reinforcer is anything that initiates or sustains a behaviour, and it can be positive or negative (see Table 1.2).

Reinforcers must be something pupils like, value or find interesting, and they can include the mere pleasure of engaging with a task for its own intrinsic sake or self-reinforcement. Whilst some pupils will make extra effort to behave as required in order to gain a pencil others will not, but they may do so for the 'privilege' of sharpening pencils for their teacher. For some pupils,

Table 1.2 Positive and negative reinforcement

Type of reinforcement	Description	Outcomes	Example
Positive reinforcement	Add or increase a pleasant stimulus	Behaviour is strengthened	Giving a pupil a prize after she gets an A on a test
Negative reinforcement	Reduce or remove an unpleasant stimulus	Behaviour is strengthened	Allow pupils to miss homework to watch a 'special' TV show increases the likelihood that they will request this again

just being in a particular teacher's classroom is sufficient to motivate them to engage with learning and behave as that teacher requires. House points or merits given for behaving as required are potential reinforcers for some, but not all pupils. So you need to know your pupils: what they like and do not like; what their interests are both in and out of school; what types of lessons and which subjects they find most and least interesting and so on. Knowing this provides you with information to initiate and sustain engagement with their learning. A simple way of finding this out is to use the 'All about me' questionnaire (see Chapter 10), which is quick and easy to administer to a class and can be reviewed at your leisure.

Reinforcers are divided into primary (e.g. food) or secondary (e.g. stickers) (see Table 1.3) and they range from tangible (e.g. food) to abstract (e.g. praise). However, praise can be both effective and ineffective, so it needs to be used thoughtfully. Burnett and Mandel (2010) found that general, non-targeted praise was the type of praise most frequently used by teachers (77% of lessons) despite general praise being shown *not* to be predictive of a positive classroom environment or of having a positive relationship with a teacher (Burnett, 2002). Over several decades, many researchers (e.g. Brophy, 1981; Gable *et al.*, 2009; Lannie and McCurdy, 2007) have found that praise is ineffective

Table 1.3 Types and categories of reinforcer

Type	Category	Examples
Primary reinforcers	Edible Sensory	Food Music
Secondary reinforcers	Tangible Special activities Responsibilities Social	Stickers Computer time Monitor Verbal feedback

unless contingent on a specific behaviour. A statement such as 'Filip, I am impressed by the way you are working on your drawing', is more effective than a vague statement such as 'great job'. Praise can also negatively affect learning. Hyland and Hyland (2006) found that around 50% of teachers' feedback was praise, but also noted that premature and gratuitous praise confused pupils and discouraged persistence, especially when they began to fail on a task. The most harmful effect of praise is that it can feed learned helplessness (Chapter 7) because pupils come to depend on being praised in order to engage with their learning. Providing pupils with feedback without praise led to more engagement and effort than feedback with praise (Kessels *et al.*, 2008).

With social behaviour, Loveless (1996) found praise was most effective when it was delivered immediately and enthusiastically, when it involved eye contact with a pupil, when it *specified* behaviour and when a range of praise statements were used (Burnett, 2002). However, when a teacher says 'well done' to different pupils, despite intending to communicate the same sentiment to them all, because vocal tones differ on each occasion, praise may be interpreted subjectively. In contrast, giving someone a token does not suffer from this subjective effect (Kazadin, 1977).

Some schools use the same reward for the same behaviour *ad infinitum* despite even the most attractive reward losing its impact or value over time. Whilst the initial novelty may attract the desired behaviour, any reward loses its effectiveness if used repeatedly over time. Think of your favourite food and imagine having it for every meal, every day, for a month – would you not welcome a change? The important message here is to review and vary reinforcers over time (Stafford *et al.*, 2002).

Getting pupils to manage their own behaviour

The long-term objective should be to move pupils from external reinforcement towards regulating their own behaviour. However, the time this takes will vary depending on a range of factors, not least the level of self-control your pupils have when you begin teaching them. In the early stages. external reinforcement should be continuous, gradually moving to intermittent over time, and *always* contingent on a pupil or group displaying the required behaviour; otherwise, it will be less effective. The easiest way to manage this in a planned way is to produce a reinforcement schedule (see Figure 10.5). A schedule has two broad elements, continuous and intermittent reinforcement. Continuous reinforcement is where reinforcement is provided whenever the target behaviour occurs. Intermittent reinforcement is where reinforcement is provided after *some* behaviours, but not every time.

Whilst continuous reinforcement is commonly used to establish new behaviours, intermittent reinforcement is used to maintain previously learned behaviours (Cooper *et al.*, 2007). To establish a new behaviour or routine, or to motivate a disengaged class, it is usual to begin by using a regular reinforcement system (Alberto and Troutman, 2013) to encourage them to engage with learning. If at this stage teachers are inconsistent in their reinforcement of the behaviour they require, pupils become uncertain of what is expected of them (Evertson *et al.*, 2003). However, once initial learning has been achieved through continuous reinforcement, intermittent reinforcement produces stronger learning (Cameron, 2002). Consider for example, how people are motivated to continue putting money into a slot machine, even though they do not know when they will win – but know that it is possible.

There are four basic forms of intermittent reinforcement:

- *Fixed-ratio reinforcement schedule*—Reinforcement is provided after a 'fixed' number of correct responses (e.g. completing five maths problems).
- *Variable-ratio reinforcement schedule*—Reinforcement frequency will 'vary', e.g. a teacher will reinforce following one correct response, then after three correct responses, then five, then two and so on.
- *Fixed-interval reinforcement schedule*—Reinforcement will be available after a specific period of time (e.g. staying on task for five minutes).
- *Variable-interval reinforcement schedule*—Specific varying periods of time must be met before reinforcement becomes available (e.g. sometimes after five minutes on task, sometimes after ten minutes).

Sometimes different schedule regimes are operated concurrently and in conjunction with different reinforcers, so verbal support may be used at fixed intervals, whereas tokens (e.g. stickers) are used on a more variable schedule. The sooner reinforcement is given following performance of the desired behaviour, the greater the effect on that behaviour since 'those responses that precede the reinforcer most closely in time are strengthened the most' (Donahoe and Dorsel, 1999: 273). Not doing so results in a weak association between behaviour and consequence. Finally, reinforcers should not cost a lot of money, nor require a lot of staff time or effort to administer (Rhode *et al.*, 1996).

Ignoring an undesirable behaviour *may* result in reducing or stopping it (extinction), depending upon what is reinforcing the behaviour. If receiving attention for misbehaving is reinforcing, then starving the pupil of that attention may reduce it. On the other hand, it may result in pupils using more extreme behaviour to gain attention, which cannot be ignored.

Rewards and pupil motivation

Some argue that pupils should not be rewarded for behaving in a socially acceptable way. However, there is considerable empirical evidence that teachers who do not offer rewards to pupils for behaving as required run the risk of creating a negative classroom climate, and increased antagonism towards school (Colvin, 2004; Evertson *et al.*, 2003; Kauffman, 2008).

The positive effects on GCSE performance of using extrinsic motivation, in the form of financial and non-financial incentives for low-attaining pupils, was demonstrated in a recent field study. Burgess *et al.* (2016) measured the performance of 10,600 pupils taking GCSEs at more than 60 secondary schools. They found that although the incentives had limited impact on stronger students, underachieving pupils improved their exam grades and pass rates by up to 10%.

Deci *et al.* (1999) had argued that extrinsic rewards for *learning* reduces the motivation to learn for its own sake. Other researchers have demonstrated that rewards can increase intrinsic motivation (Cameron *et al.*, 2005). In their analysis of 145 studies, Pierce *et al.* (2003) found that *contingent* rewards, i.e. *only* given for completing a *specific* task to a required standard, had a positive effect on intrinsic motivation, which was maintained or enhanced when the rewards were given for meeting a specific criterion. A few very rare circumstances where rewards were not effective were when: 1) the pupil was already highly engaged with a task, 2) the reward was a tangible item, and 3) the reward was given without reference to a specific behaviour. When these three conditions occurred, output decreased – but this did *not* happen when the reward was unexpected. There is now acceptance among most researchers that motivation is driven by both intrinsic and extrinsic elements at any given time, and both forms can occur simultaneously (Covington and Müeller, 2001).

Chance, commenting on whether it is right or wrong to reward pupils for positive behaviour in school said:

> ...If it is immoral ... to pat students on the back for a good effort, to show joy at a student's understanding of a concept, or to recognise the achievement of a goal by providing a gold star or a certificate – if this is immoral, then count me a sinner.
>
> (1993: 788)

To maximise the effect and approach of this process in an objective way, you should plan your reinforcement schedule in advance and monitor effectiveness, adjusting the rate of reinforcement in response to measured effect.

Punishment

Many schools prefer to use terms like 'sanctions' or 'consequences', considering the term 'punishment' to have negative connotations (Robertson, 1996). For pupils on the receiving end, the semantics are less important than the actions. Unfortunately, many schools employ more punishment-based practices (e.g. classroom exclusion and suspensions), than rewards for positive behaviour (Maag, 2001). Despite perhaps making schools seem safer by removing those pupils who exhibit the most severe challenging behaviours, such measures fail to teach these pupils how to behave in more socially acceptable ways (ibid.).

In behavioural approaches, punishment has a technical definition that describes a relationship between specific *mis*behaviour and a consequence which must reduce the likelihood of its reoccurrence (Alberto and Troutman, 2013). As with reinforcement, punishment can be positive or negative (see Table 1.4).

Actions in response to unacceptable behaviour are not punishment just because someone thinks the consequence is unpleasant. To qualify as punishment a response should be *contingent* on the demonstration of a particular behaviour and result in that behaviour decreasing. Furthermore, to be most effective, punishment should occur as near to the behaviour as possible to help the recipient to associate the link between the two. Punishing pupils by putting them in detention on Friday for something they did on Monday morning does not meet this criterion. Furthermore, psychological and neuroscientific research has shown that adolescents tend to focus on the present, giving little thought to how their actions will affect their future outcomes (e.g. Bettinger and Slonim, 2007; Gruber and Yurgelun-Todd, 2005; Steinberg *et al.*, 2009).

A punishment is only ever a punishment if it reduces or stops the undesirable behaviour – if it does not do so, it is not a punishment. For example, if a teacher repeatedly sends a pupil out of class for refusing to work and the pupil continues to misbehave, then sending out is not a punishment. Whilst the miscreant's absence provides respite for teacher and class, it is doing nothing to teach her/him the required behaviour (Maag, 2001). The pupil has probably learnt an association between the misbehaviour and being allowed to wander round outside the classroom. Since the pupil is avoiding the aversive experience, he/she is likely to continue misbehaving to achieve his/her aim – this is negative reinforcement (see Table 1.2).

Punishment is much more readily accepted in schools for many reasons, as it can terminate unacceptable behaviour quickly. However, it is often only temporary and only in the presence of the punisher, e.g. the familiar practice in some schools of a senior member of staff sitting in with an NQT for 'support', resulting in better behaviour until the senior member

Table 1.4 Positive and negative punishments

Type of punishment	Description	Outcomes	Example
Positive punishment	Present or add an unpleasant stimulus	Behaviour is weakened	Giving a pupil extra homework after she misbehaves in class
Negative punishment	Reduce or remove a pleasant stimulus	Behaviour is weakened	Preventing a pupil going to football practice because of misbehaviour

leaves. Behaviour management based on punishment is preferred to positive reinforcement since the latter is more time-consuming and more complex (Axelrod, 1996). Nonetheless, you would (I assume) find it odd if I were to say the most effective way to motivate pupils to engage with your academic subject is to punish anyone who produced the wrong answer. And yet that is how many teachers operate in respect of social behaviour – pupils are expected to behave, and if they do not they are punished. I am not suggesting that pupils who misbehave should not be punished; however, it is not the way to teach pupils how to behave. The best that punishment achieves is how to avoid punishment.

The brain uses separate systems to process rewards and threats (punishment), which affects subsequent behaviour – rewards facilitating learning, threats inhibiting it. There are also developmental differences in the effects of reward and punishment on brain activity that are age-related. Crone et al. (2005, 2014) found that children responded disproportionately to punishment. They argued that, whilst reward is more effective than punishment, the latter is less effective with younger and developmentally delayed children, because failure is more complicated and requires more effortful thinking to understand than success. It necessitates more deliberate conscious activity to pursue causal explanations for failure, and younger pupils are still developing the mechanisms that control this.

In sum, positive reinforcement of pupils for completing required tasks is more effective in improving the overall behaviour of all pupils in classrooms. It is proactive and aims to teach pupils what they should do – that is, they should behave in a socially responsible way. In contrast, punishment teaches them what they should *not* do. Many behaviourists believe that behavioural approaches represent the only way to maintain control over pupils' learning (Alberto and Troutman, 2013). It is the teacher who manipulates the environment to bring about behaviour change in the pupil (Wheldall and Merrett, 1984). However, in some settings, pupils are involved in the process.

Teachers should adopt approaches where the weight of evidence from research support it, and behavioural approaches have received solid support in the literature for decades (e.g. Fabiano et al., 2009; Stage and Quiroz, 1997).

Cognitive behavioural approaches (CBA)

CBA utilise behavioural methods to change overt behaviour alongside self-directed change of covert behaviours (cognition) (Larson and Lochman, 2003). CBA are not informed by a single coalesced theory. They are represented by a loose collection of models and methods arranged around the premise that emotions and associated behaviours result from a transaction between the environment and a pupil's interpretation and appraisal of it – which can be positive or negative (Friedberg and McClure, 2002). The following sections examine a number of the theories, models and methods.

A large number of studies have demonstrated CBA effectiveness in managing disruptive and aggressive behaviours in schoolchildren. For reviews, see Ho *et al.*, 2010; Mennuti *et al.*, 2012; Sukhodolsky *et al.*, 2004; Weisz and Kazdin, 2010.

CBA utilise two interacting approaches – cognitive and behavioural – to produce tailored responses to address a behaviour issue (Kendall, 2000). They can be operated at the group level (whole class) or individual level (aggressive pupil). The behavioural element addresses the environmental effects (e.g. seating arrangements) and/or skills deficits (e.g. social skills). Cognitive elements address either cognitive deficiencies (e.g. underdeveloped impulse control) or cognitive distortions (e.g. misinterpreting social cues) (Kendall and MacDonald, 1993).

The balance between cognitive and behavioural elements used depends on the developmental level of the pupil. Given the emphasis on language in cognitive approaches, pupils with limited language development will require a larger behavioural element. Another consideration is that cognitive elements rely on an established positive relationship between teacher and pupils since they require active interaction in a safe and trusting environment in order to empower pupils (Beck, 1995). Finally, pupils need to have the motivation to change.

What distinguishes CBA from purely behavioural approaches is that, whilst acknowledging the power of direct reinforcement on behaviour, people are able to learn by observing others being rewarded for their behaviour, which they then imitate in anticipation of being likewise rewarded. Furthermore, it is accepted that there exists a reciprocal relationship between behaviour, the environment and cognition, so CBA extend the behavioural approach to recognise internal processing and personal agency. The interconnection between your thoughts, feelings, physical sensations and actions means that getting locked into negative thoughts and feelings can draw you into a negative behavioural cycle.

Social cognitive theory

Bandura (2001) argued that direct reinforcement of behaviour could not explain all forms of learning. Whilst experiencing reinforcement and punishment directly plays an important role in motivation and learning, observing others being reinforced or punished can also be motivating and bring about behaviour change. Bandura (1986) proposed a social cognitive theory (SCT), with emphasis on social influence alongside external and internal reinforcement and highlighting the importance of self-reflection and self-regulation in determining ongoing behaviour. As Bandura and Locke put it, in SCT 'people function as anticipative, purposive, and self-evaluating proactive regulators of their motivation and actions' (2003: 87).

Bandura proposed a reciprocal relationship between personal factors (e.g. cognition), behaviour, and environmental factors (e.g. school), all of

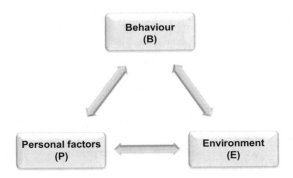

Figure 1.2 Triadic reciprocity – the relationship between personal factors, the environment and behaviour.

which influence each other bi-directionally, something he called triadic reciprocal determinism (see Figure 1.2). In doing so, he challenged previous explanations, which he referred to as unidirectional, i.e. human behaviour is generated from *either* internal processes or external processes.

However, he did not suggest that all three factors have equal weight, nor that they all operate simultaneously. Personal factors: including what people think, feel, believe and expect; their goals; and their physical make-up influence how they behave. Their behaviour is then responded to by others (the environment), which may lead to them thinking or feeling differently about themselves (positively or negatively). The same behaviour praised in one context may receive admonishment in another – shouting on a football field is likely to be viewed differently to shouting in a library. People also display different social reactions to others, depending on their social status. For example, a pupil who has a reputation as being aggressive will likely provoke different reactions from peers and teachers than someone considered shy or withdrawn. Sometimes their reputation can affect their environment without them saying or doing anything. Changing a single element of the triad can have a knock-on effect on the other elements. For example, changing your teaching style (E) may result in increased on-task activity of a usually disruptive pupil (B), which may lead to that pupil enjoying learning and success (P). Alternatively, taking action to get a pupil to think differently about behaviour (P) may lead to a change in their behaviour (B), which may change the classroom climate (E).

Self-efficacy

Bandura (2001) argued that through personal agency individuals can influence and regulate their own behaviour (self-regulation) and their environment in a focused, goal-directed way. Personal agency is an individual's belief in their capability to originate and direct actions. It is influenced by the belief that you have the capability to complete tasks (self-efficacy). Research over the last 40 years has demonstrated that pupils' self-efficacy is a powerful predictor of achievement, how much effort they expend, how long they persist and their resilience in the face of adversity (Pajares and Urban, 2006). Pupils who doubt, or are uncertain about their capabilities, are most likely to disengage from learning and engage in disruptive behaviour.

Self-efficacy can be measured at different levels, from the specific (your beliefs about your ability to teach science) to more global (your beliefs about your ability to influence school policy). It is dynamic and influenced by context. Consider the difference between being asked to teach a class which you believe is likely to be extremely difficult to manage, with one where you believe the pupils are extremely well-behaved. Self-efficacy is not the same as self-esteem, which is the degree to which you like yourself. Teachers often try to boost the self-esteem of pupils who are struggling using general praise e.g. 'You did really well'. Whilst soothing children who appear upset with comments believed to enhance self-esteem seems natural, they do not promote self-efficacy. Levels of self-efficacy depend on four factors: mastery experiences (past experiences), vicarious experiences (modelling by others), verbal persuasion (feedback, teaching), physiological feedback (emotional state) (Bandura, 1997).

- *Mastery experiences*, according to Bandura:

> Enactive mastery experiences are the most influential source of efficacy information because they provide the most authentic evidence of whether one can muster whatever it takes to succeed. Success builds a robust belief in one's personal efficacy. Failures undermine it, especially if failures occur before a sense of efficacy is firmly established.
>
> However, some difficulties and setbacks serve a beneficial purpose in teaching that success usually requires sustained effort.

(1997: 80)

Coping with setbacks provides opportunities for learning how to turn failure into success by refining people's capabilities to have improved control over important events and resilience.
- *Vicarious experiences*, or observing others who are similar to oneself succeeding on a task, can reinforce a belief that we too can influence our environment.
- *Verbal persuasion*, for example feedback, should be frequent and focused and not general praise, as discussed earlier. Comparisons should be made to the pupils' own not peers' performance to develop mastery thinking.
- *Emotional state* (and trait) can have a profound impact on self-efficacy. In social contexts, the presence of others can be facilitatory or inhibitory.

41

The latter is often linked to high aversive arousal, which can be debilitating, for example, being observed teaching an unfamiliar subject. The opposite being the case with a subject in which you have expertise. Emotional experiences include the interpretation and appraisal of a physiological state (sweating, tense) which is influenced by the situation. Emotional self-efficacy involves taking ownership of one's feelings and understanding that emotions are subjective and do not reflect objective facts. Many emotions reflect social labels, so modelling and teaching pupils to regulate their emotions and express emotions appropriate to the circumstance in a socially acceptable way is important.

Self-efficacy is not the same as confidence. Bandura stated that 'Confidence is a nondescript term that refers to strength of belief but does not necessarily specify what the certainty is about' (1997: 382). Outcome expectations are also important in SCT because they influence people's decisions about what action to take and what to withhold. Where outcome expectations are salient, individuals are likely to make an effort but avoid doing so where they are not. Self-efficacy beliefs influence how individuals regulate their own behaviour. Shonkoff and Phillips (2000) consider self-regulation to be the foundation of children's development influencing all aspects of behaviour. Self-regulation is the basis for choice, decision making and for control of higher cognitive processes. Unfortunately, some pupils will not have fully developed these self-regulatory skills by the time they reach secondary school.

Modelling behaviour

Bandura promoted the concept of vicarious reinforcement – whereby an individual, observing someone being rewarded for behaving in a particular way (modelling) encodes that relationship and then copies the behaviour in anticipation of achieving a similar outcome. In a classroom, a pupil observing another pupil receiving positive comment from the teacher for raising their hand to ask a question, may well copy that behaviour (assuming they value the positive comment from the teacher) in anticipation of being similarly reinforced. Pupils also learn unacceptable behaviours in the same way. A pupil, observing a classmate causing others to laugh by being rude to the teacher, may well present similar behaviour to get the class to laugh. It follows then that adults should be aware of what they are modelling to pupils, both intended and unintended.

Aggressive behaviour is a case in point. Bandura *et al.* (1961) showed how aggressive behaviour can be reinforced through observational learning. He went on to claim that exposing children to antisocial models in the media, home, local community and school should be of concern to responsible adults.

Bandura and colleagues carried out a series of classic experiments with children using a Bobo Doll (an inflatable toy standing around 150cm high, made of plastic and usually painted to look clown-like. It is bottom-weighted, so if hit, it falls over but returns immediately to an upright position). In his experiments, children observed adults hitting the Bobo Doll. In one experiment (Bandura *et al.*, 1961) a group of boys and girls observed an adult in a playroom punching a Bobo Doll and hitting it with a mallet. Later, the children, along with the control group, were left in a room full of toys including a Bobo Doll. Children, both boys and girls, who had seen an adult assaulting a Bobo Doll were more aggressive towards the doll (especially those who witnessed same sex adult models) than the control group who had not witnessed the aggression. A second experiment (Bandura *et al.*, 1963) followed a similar theme, except that the children observed videos of the adult aggression to the doll. In one video, the adult was rewarded after assaulting the doll; in a second, the adult was punished after doing so and in the third, the adult received neither punishment nor reward. Following the videos, the children were left in a room full of toys including a Bobo Doll. Children, both boys and girls, who had seen the adult being rewarded showed the highest levels of aggression, whereas those who had seen the adult being punished showed less aggression than either of the other conditions. Bandura carried out many variations of the experiment (e.g. using a live clown) and found similar results. As with all psychological research, the work was criticised for using an experimental method as opposed to 'real' life representation of violence (Wortman *et al.*, 1998). However, debates about the influence of exposure to violence on children and young people's behaviour – in the home, community and through violent media – continue. A wealth of research findings confirm that children (mainly boys) exposed to media violence have increased probability of aggression (Anderson *et al.*, 2003). Eron *et al.* (1972) found relationship between having viewed television violence during early childhood and aggressive and antisocial behaviour ten years later.

Longitudinal studies of children's development, using large samples, have consistently shown that the peak age for aggression is between the age of three and four years – the best time to intervene and prevent the development of chronic aggression (Tremblay, 2007). Although most children learn to regulate their emotions and begin developing a repertoire of socially acceptable coping responses from then on, some do not even by secondary school (see also Chapter 9).

Condon (2002) argued that advertising for violent movies, television shows, video games, and music CDs deliberately targets young audiences who develop aggressive and violent scripts (Bushman and Huesmann, 2006). Cognitive scripts provide a blueprint of what is likely to happen, how to respond and likely outcomes. To understand scripts, think about the sequence of events when going into a restaurant: being greeted, directed to a table, offered a menu etc. Children exposed to violent images develop cognitive scripts which are stored in the memory and act as guides to social problem-solving (Abelson, 1981). As a result, they failed to develop non-aggressive coping strategies to deal with frustration and regulation of their thoughts and feelings. This limited and aggressively loaded repertoire of responses was linked to persistent long-term aggressive behaviours and beliefs (ibid.).

Children and adolescents have an innate tendency to imitate the behaviour of people they observe (Hurley and Chatter, 2004), action which neuroscientists attribute to 'mirror neurons' (Rizzolatti *et al.*, 1996). Observing violence can be arousing as defined by physiological measures such as heart rate, blood pressure etc. This arousal makes the activation of an established coping strategy more likely, which, in the case of those with aggressive tendencies, often leads to more aggression (Berkowitz, 1993). Following arousal, the residual negative emotion (mild anger) can later make responses to minor events more exaggerated through excitation transfer (Zillmann *et al.*, 1981), i.e. they react even more aggressively.

In sum, pupils who observe aggressive behaviour are likely to reproduce aggressive behaviour (e.g. Anderson *et al.*, 2003), and repeated viewing of violent images desensitises attitudes towards violence. Desensitisation is a process where emotional arousal is lowered, in this case, when exposed to aggression. Based on physiological measures (heart rate and respiration), Staude-Müller *et al.* (2008) found that individuals exposed to violent, as opposed to non-violent, video games were found to have lower levels of emotional arousal when subsequently exposed to further violent images.

However, whist modelling has been shown to have negative outcomes, it is also an effective way of teaching pupils how to behave both academically and socially. But to ensure its effectiveness requires attention to the following four elements of modelling which make behaviour change most likely (Bandura, 1997):

- *Attention*—Attention is influenced by many factors (e.g. emotional significance; distinctiveness; complexity). Pupils easily distracted can have problems with observational learning.
- *Retention*—The ability to remember what you have observed, along with the ability to store the information, requires mental imaging, cognitive organisation and symbolic representations of the modelled behaviour. So, an individual constructs a cognitive model of what he/she has observed and then rehearses it mentally to produce an enduring mental model – essential if the behaviour is to be repeated in the absence of the model. Hence, to ensure behaviour modelled to your class is sustained in your absence requires the pupils to have developed such a model.
- *Reproduction*—Copying and practicing motor components and integrating them in order to develop the skills, patterns and sequences required to reproduce the observed behaviour.
- *Motivation*—There must be a desire to perform the task for intrinsic or extrinsic value based on previous success (reinforcement), expectation of receiving reinforcement or seeing someone else being reinforced for demonstrating that behaviour.

Modelling is more likely to be copied when performed by someone you trust and with whom you have a positive relationship. Using modelling as a teaching tool in a planned way, a teacher is able to demonstrate correct social protocols when speaking, and through nonverbal behaviours (gesture, posture, personal space, etc.) to indicate positive and negative responses and emotional reactions. At the same time teachers should be aware of the potential negative effects of modelling by antisocial peers who model and 'reward' antisocial and delinquent behaviour (Patterson *et al.*, 1990).

Inner speech and self-regulation

The basic premise in cognitive approaches is that people's difficulties are rooted in their beliefs, expectations, interpretations and evaluations of their worlds (Corey, 1986). Distorted interpretations lead to negative thinking, negative emotions and behaviour difficulties. Negative thinking is likely to generate self-defeating behaviours ('I'm useless, so why bother trying') and CBA work toward changing this inner speech and thus behaviour. CBA focus on promoting positive feelings through using language to alter cognitive processes (e.g. perception, beliefs and social problem-solving) which in turn change behaviour. Distorted cognitive processes, such as faulty social information processing, contribute to the maintenance of behavioural problems.

There are various forms of CBA to address negative and distorted cognition and self-defeating behaviour including: conflict resolution; anger management; social problem-solving; self-instructional training – which are used in the treatment of disruptive behaviour disorders (Beck and Fernandez, 1998). All are based on the belief that as pupils progress through school they should be capable of regulating their emotions, delaying gratification, being reflective in their decision making, and developing their social competence to cope with different social contexts.

One approach, self-instruction training (SIT), is used to train pupils to develop self-control using modelling and guided self-talk. SIT has proved to be effective in increasing prosocial behaviour (Camp *et al.*, 1977) and decreasing distractibility, aggressiveness, and restlessness (Kendall, 1982; Kendall and Zupan, 1981). The emphasis is on teaching children *how* to think rather than *what* to think. In SIT, the emphasis is on teaching children how to use verbal mediation to initiate and guide behaviour. Meichenbaum (1977) developed a five-stage model of SIT (see Table 1.5) which has proven successful in helping children to control their own behaviour (e.g. impulsivity). Manning (1991) provides a detailed account of the processes, including classroom applications. SIT owes much to the Russian psychologists Vygotsky and Luria, who theorised how the origins of thought are in 'external processes of social life, in the social and historical forms of human existence' (Luria, 1981: 25). For Vygotsky, children are born with some inherited capabilities, such as perception, attention, memory and basic emotions, which are

Table 1.5 Procedural steps in self-instruction training used with individual pupil or group of pupils

Step	Behaviour
1. Cognitive modelling	Adult models the behaviour whilst saying aloud what they are doing
2. Overt external guidance	The behaviour is copied by the pupils with overt adult guidance
3. Overt self-guidance	The behaviour is performed by the pupils whilst saying the instructions out loud
4. Faded overt self-guidance	The behaviour is performed by the pupils whilst whispering instructions
5. Covert self-guidance	The behaviour is performed by the pupils with silent self-guidance – speech is internalised

transformed through socialisation and education to generate higher-order mental functions. A child begins with a focus on concrete stimuli in their immediate environment then moves towards self-formulated goals through the development of self-regulatory skills.

Luria (1971) proposed that children's behaviour is subject to Pavlov's 'rule of force' (the strongest stimulus will win), and the child responds to its carer's speech like any other stimulus. As the child develops, speech becomes the dominant force – provided there is no conflict between mother's speech and the child's activity, in which case the latter will win. Pupils who have established verbal control over their behaviour are able to follow verbal requests even in the presence of other potentially distracting environmental stimuli. However, some pupils in secondary schools will find this difficult, notably those with attention deficits. Prior to establishing such control, there is a *zone of potential development* wherein the child may exercise control using their own overt speech. Finally, an older child will utilise covert or inner speech to control their 'voluntary behaviour' (Luria, 1961). Vygotsky (1978) proposed that every function in a child's psychological development occurs twice. First, at the social level (or interpsychological) and second, within the child (or intrapsychological). The interpsychological involves the transmission of socio-cultural tools (e.g. language) from others to the child, which he/she adopts initially to serve solely as social functions or ways to communicate needs. Vygotsky believed that the internalisation of speech led to higher thinking skills (e.g. planning, decision making and self-control) or the ability to guide our actions in the service of a particular goal. There is considerable empirical evidence to support Vygotsky's claims about the development of verbal self-regulation being mediated through social interaction (Winsler *et al.*, 2009).

Executive functioning and impulse control

Executive functioning (EF) sometimes used interchangeably with self-regulation (or BOSS, Chapter 2) is a catchall term that refers to higher-order, 'supervisory' mental structures, which control complex thoughts and behaviour. These structures enable individuals to maintain focus and solve problems in the presence of distractions and involve working memory, planning and goal-setting. Carlson and Moses (2001) considered EF development to be the growing ability to inhibit inappropriate behaviour, whilst Case (1996) felt it was how well an individual could draw on various types of information to plan and monitor their actions.

EF is a theorised cognitive system, but evidence from neuroimaging now suggests that EF is intimately connected with the frontal lobes of the brain. According to Luria (1973), EF development is driven by maturation of the prefrontal cortex in the first five years of life. Vocabulary is strongly connected to executive function (Hongwanishkul et al., 2005), and research evidence highlights a relationship between poor language skills and physical aggression. Given the interpersonal nature of aggression, it is little wonder that language skills are particularly important for regulating social interaction (Séguin et al., 2009). Individuals at any age, with limited language skills are more likely to have a limited linguistic and behavioural repertoire, so they resort to physical aggression when under pressure. EF, or lack of it, plays an important role in the development of behaviour disorders (Castellanos et al., 2006; Sonuga-Barke, 2005; Seguin et al., 2004).

In typical social development, individuals learn to regulate their impulses and delay gratification through internalised self-statements. This is a natural process when a child is raised in a social facilitatory environment, where carers take the time to direct and correct behaviour, which eventually becomes internalised. In atypical development (e.g. impulsive-aggressive individuals), the inability to regulate behaviour is often because of distorted social information processing whereby neutral social signals are misinterpreted as being potential threats (Choe et al., 2015). Impulsive-aggressive children and adolescents can be very demanding, leading to carers seeking respite, which can lead to children spending too much time isolated, playing computer games, for instance. Where the games are violent, the negative effects are exacerbated. Video games, whilst providing instant and continuous reinforcement (i.e. no need to delay gratification), lack social interaction and subsequently the development of inner speech – self-instruction training can be used to correct this.

Whilst emphasising the salience of language in the transmission of cultural knowledge, Vygotsky (1962) also recognised that some things are better learned through observation. He saw the ability to imitate as an important sign that a child was developmentally ready to understand a particular task (in the same way, Bandura viewed the role of modelling in social development).

In sum, the approaches reviewed above all acknowledge the importance of external and internal forces on behaviour but differ in the way they believe these forces operate. All have proven effective at changing behaviour but differ in their fundamental assumptions about where to begin with an intervention. In deciding which to adopt at any one point depends on the nature of the behaviour problem and developmental level of target pupils (e.g. language level, social development, self-awareness) and the quality of the teacher–pupil and pupil–pupil relationships. Teachers should adopt approaches which have the strongest level of empirical evidence to support them. CBA have received solid and consistent support for many decades.

Annotated further reading

Porter, L. (2006). *Behaviour in schools: theory and practice for teachers.* Buckingham: Open University Press.

Porter describes a range of theories and approaches relating to managing behaviour. She discusses their underlying philosophy, understanding of childhood, practical application and case studies and highlights the assumptions, effectiveness and different goals of each.

Further reading to support M level study

Martella, R., Nelson, J., Marchand-Martella, N., and O'Reilly, M. (2012). *Comprehensive behavior management* (2nd ed.). Thousand Oaks, CA: Sage.

Part I: Introduction to behaviour management

The first part of this book reviews eight different classroom management models and offers a critique of both positive and negative features of each model. All eight models have their origins, however tenuous, in psychological theories or their author's interpretation of those theories in terms of how they might apply to managing behaviour in the classroom. Whilst all eight models have positive elements and are used in some schools, several have little (if any) evidence to support their effectiveness beyond sounding like a nice idea.

9 Managing student behaviour

Our students crave confidence and trust in their teacher. They seek it out, listening for it in the words we speak and looking to read it in our every gesture and movement.

We send out messages all day long that are stored and accumulated by our students. Our students loathe mixed messages. When we say 'Any questions?' but we then don't pause and wait for a response because we don't really want any questions, our students lose a degree of trust. Each and every interaction makes up our relationship, and that relationship can define the behaviour of our students.

The craving our students exhibit for confidence and trust in their teacher is largely grown from our being caring and consistent.

We can create a safe classroom that is founded on trust and care, yet we know that students can face battles outside of school that drain their capacity to trust. Every once in a while the bleak personal stories of our students' lives are opened up to us like a drawer of knives. We get a brief glimpse into personal prisons that children shouldn't ever experience.

Many of our students' negative behaviours in our classroom become better understood when we hear their story: the missing homework, the rudeness, the mood swings, or the inability to look us in the eye when we speak to them. It never excuses the damaging behaviours that they commit, with other children often caught in the middle of those vicious salvos, but it does illuminate and explain their origins.

I think about a recent student of mine: let's call her Jessica for the sake of her privacy. Only recently I heard the latest update about her life since leaving school. To describe her family as 'broken' would not do justice to the chaos it had wrought upon her young self, and continued to do, beyond her removal from school.

I was reminded of the mix of emotions I felt when she left my class. My instinctive feeling that I had personally failed her was mingled with guilt for being somewhat relieved at her permanently leaving my class. I had momentarily feasted on the optimism that a change of setting, and school, could better suit her needs; that a new school would provide her with a fresh start.

Predictably, a rumoured update about Jessica laid waste to my hopes.

We do our very best each day for students like Jessica, despite the most trying of circumstances. We give them unconditional regard; we set the boundaries they have needed all along; we attempt to lift them with our rocket-high expectations. Despite this, the complex circumstances in the lives of our students like Jessica undermine our attempts to improve their behaviour and to develop their confidence. They inhibit the capacity for trust in us as a teacher: a chief ingredient in providing the conditions for developing a successful relationship.

In 1974, the eminent psychologist Walter Mischel conducted a famous experiment: *The Marshmallow Test*. Two fluffy cubes of sugar would come to symbolise a child's capacity for self-control. It was a simply designed test: a child was given one marshmallow. They were sat in a room for a short time and if they could fend off eating the single marshmallow then they were granted a second marshmallow as a reward. It was a classic exercise in impulse control and delayed gratification.

For children like Jessica, her environment was so unstable that she would struggle to not eat the marshmallow. The patent lack of stability and trust in her life would likely see her impulses take control, possibly imitating some of the damaging behaviours from her chaotic home life.

Celeste Kidd, a researcher from the University of Rochester, imitated Mischel's classic marshmallow test. Her study on 'rational snacking'[1] showed that when the people giving the marshmallows proved unreliable, then children were more likely to eat the marshmallow. This simple experiment exposed a profound human truth: trust can drive our behaviour. It certainly influences the behaviour of our students.

It follows that when we are considering the best behaviour management of our students, each teacher should ask: how will I earn the trust of my students? What actions will I undertake with fairness and consistency?

You may rightly question: what about those students who misbehave despite the best circumstances in their home lives? Frankly, there are many more of these students than there are students who are suffering from bad fortune like Jessica. And yet, the core principles of confident behaviour management remain the same for all students, in any classroom:

- Students need a teacher who is consistent, reliable and trustworthy.
- They need a teacher who develops a relationship founded upon trust.
- They need a teacher who calmly and consistently models the behaviours they expect.
- They need a teacher who relentlessly makes their high expectations of behaviour clear to all.

In short, all students need *confidence* in their teacher.

Just like adults, and teachers, self-confident students better persevere and maintain their effort through difficulties and challenges.[2] What develops between the teacher and the student becomes a relationship built upon reciprocity – we share confidence in one another.

Developing relationships with our students is of course our first priority. We can then establish a climate of trust without a reliance on fear. This isn't necessarily about proving ourselves as their new favourite teacher. Too easily, a focus on trust and developing a relationship becomes confused with being liked and not establishing the boundaries for the good behaviour that are needed. The kindest act we could ever commit for our students would be to give them the safety conferred by explicit boundaries of how they should behave.

We are ultimately their role models in their school lives and beyond. We face the marshmallow test of self-control each day too. When we are stressed, tired and strained by over-work, we need to maintain our consistency, our control and our self-confidence.

If we are to manage the behaviour of others successfully, we must first be successful in managing our own. This necessitates being consciously aware of our language, the non-verbal messages we convey along with our words, as well as possessing an acute understanding of the needs of all of our students.

We need to build rigorous and relentless routines. School-wide systems and high standards of support are crucial, but consistency begins at home. Creating clear and consistent rules sits comfortably with a climate of unmitigated regard for our students.

Confident control

It all sounds so easy. Of course, if it were so easy, then the challenging behaviour of our students would not prove so universally damaging to teacher confidence.

A common story is played out in every school, seemingly in every country. In self-defence, we attribute any student misbehaviour to our students and factors outside of our control. Anxiety about failing to manage our classroom cuts deep at our sense of pride. This is then compounded by our not asking for help. Before we know it, we can find ourselves crashing to the brink of burnout.

As we know, a strange truth about teaching is that it can prove a remarkably private, and even secretive, profession. As my former colleague and fellow English teacher, Helen Day, honestly stated: 'It is okay to come out as struggling with teaching approaches like questioning or feedback, but to be seen to do the same for behaviour management would be interpreted as weak.' As Helen describes, too many teachers are driven by fear and bury their issues.

In too many schools, teachers would fear for their jobs if they were open about the truth of the poor student behaviour in their classrooms, regardless of whether circumstances were patently against them. Even in good schools, with effective behaviour management systems and supportive school leaders, struggles are fought in quiet desperation in too many classrooms. The unofficial law of silence can wear away at our confidence.

We think that the teacher across the hallway is dealing with misbehaviour just fine, bolstered by many teachers claiming as much, in order to protect their own professional pride. Our psychological demons prey on our insecurities and our brain plays memory tricks on us. Ground down by our anxieties, we can too easily become overcome with negative stress.

In my first few years of teaching it was behaviour management, or more accurately my lack of it, that nearly cast me on the well-trodden path out of teaching. It was a terribly lonely experience, despite having friends and colleagues who provided much support. In an act of self-preservation, I limited knowledge of my struggles to as few people as possible.

With the vivid clarity of high-definition television, I can remember such instances of behavioural chaos in my classroom. One such incident was no doubt a turning point for me as a teacher.

To paint the scene would prove something of a parody of a gothic tale: rain lashing against a rickety temporary classroom and the darkness of an English winter gathering in. Late in the week, at the end of another gruelling school day, my GCSE English class were running me ragged.

My instructions were clanging into the corners of the room unheard. I made the weak assertion that each of my thirty-two students could choose whether they wanted to complete the essay writing task or not. I had virtually given up. Unsurprisingly, thirty-one students chose to talk and not take me up on the offer of writing their essay.

I slumped in my teacher chair, seriously contemplating my next career move – one most likely outside the classroom and the teaching profession. At home that night,

Managing student behaviour

I considered my next steps and whether teaching was for me. Too many failures, grinding tiredness and student misbehaviour, across the span of a few terms, had left me with little to no confidence in my ability to teach. The threads of my self-confidence had worn perilously thin and were close to breaking point.

The next day, I stood in front of the group and spoke of my deep disappointment. I then kept them all in class for an extra half hour (as the lesson was, fortuitously for me, situated directly before lunchtime) to do the work they had missed whilst chatting the afternoon before.

Every student was kept behind except one. The one student, who had chosen to work away the afternoon before, Natalie Elliott, had been spared my complaints and disappointment and she was sent off for her lunch as usual.

It is no exaggeration to say that it was Natalie's behaviour, her choosing to write her essay whilst all around her were talking away and wasting time, that gave me some small hope to cling to. I sat with the rest at lunchtime for thirty minutes in near pristine silence with the group. I gave them a talk that I had stewed over for hours the night before.

It wasn't the end of my behaviour management struggles by any means, but it was a turning point for me. Winning that small battle gave me some vital confidence to continue.

In retrospect, though I didn't realise it then, it was a crucial *expert experience*. It gave me just enough confidence to stave off burnout and to continue with committed effort through my all too frequent failures. With the value of hindsight, those memories now bolster my confidence. I now have a distinct sense of control, but it was hard earned and I was given a great deal of support along the way.

My training had dismally failed to prepare me for confidently managing the behaviour of all my classes. It would take some years, gathering that knowledge piece by piece, often in quiet desperation, scouring books about behaviour, watching every video on the topic I could find, whilst picking up vital tips from my more experienced colleagues.

Over time, I came to develop a repertoire of learnt behaviours that would become a visible manifestation of confident behaviour management.

In a pleasing plot twist to finish the misbehaviour anecdote that is so scorched on my memory, Natalie went on to great success in school. I went on to teach her A-level English Language and she proved the first of my students to score full marks in the examination. Then, nearly a decade later, she became a teacher colleague of mine.

She cannot remember one moment of that cold and wet afternoon, and now, I am sure she has her own afternoon battles to win, but I can remember it like it was yesterday.

The conditions for confident behaviour management

In Shakespeare's *Othello*, Cassio famously bewailed: 'Reputation, reputation, reputation!' Clearly, he understood the teeth-gnashing anxieties of teachers who have had their reputation stained by a difficult class. It happens to the best of us, inexperienced and experienced alike, as our teacher reputation can be won or lost each year of our teaching career.

The act of confident behaviour management begins even before students enter the room. Your reputation precedes you. It walks in and sits in the teacher's chair before you even turn the door handle.

Do you stick to the school rules and sanctions? Do you follow through with what you say will happen if students misbehave? In short, do students see you as a confident teacher? They make such judgements quickly and their decisions matter.

Managing student behaviour

If you don't stick to the known school rules, then students will act. There is nothing so certain as students smelling fear and seizing the initiative from a cowed teacher; such knowledge spreads like a virus. There is nothing so predictable as a teenager seeking out the unfairness of rules being inconsistently applied.

Alas, a reputation can take a great deal of time to establish and overnight success stories prove rare things. That being said, we can accelerate the process by conveying assurance and certainty. This can be asserted relatively quickly through a combination of physicality, a consistency of action, and an utter clarity when asserting our expectations.

I often hear teacher advice to establish the right 'climate for learning', or to build the right 'culture' for positive behaviour, or even more vague, 'you need to develop *presence*'. The problem is that such advice can prove maddeningly woolly and unhelpful. Instead, we need to chunk the notion of 'climate for learning' into something tangible that we can establish with a sequence of 'moves' – clear, consistent, and often, very physical moves.

We know that students make snap judgements about the capacity of their teacher in the blink of an eye. Simply pausing and giving students a momentary look can communicate control. Conversely, we can 'leak' our true feelings of nervousness with a quick twitch or harried movement. In this context, every one of our behaviour management moves can prove crucial.

The first move: Set the behaviour bar high

We can do this by making explicitly clear what good behaviour looks like, sounds like and feels like. Take a moment to ponder that point. It may sound simple and plain common sense, but we too often underestimate the value in doing so, explicitly and repeatedly.

Too many students simply don't know what good learning or good behaviour actually is, and we can too easily overlook this plain truth.

One strategy I have employed with my younger classes with success is to co-create with them a character that embodies the ideal student at the very beginning of the school year. At first it only cues a series of simplistic stereotypes, but when you get students to unpick the specific behaviours of such a student – how they ask questions; how they work in group situations; their physical behaviour when they are listening, etc – it builds up a picture of the behaviours you expect in a usefully concrete fashion.

The value is making such desirable behaviours real, embodied in a simple character, so that we can use that as our high bar of expected behaviour. That character can be emblazoned on the classroom wall as a reminder.

Alternatively, we can simply repeat, repeat and repeat our expectations so that good behaviour is explicit and obvious for all. It may take some valuable curriculum time to do it, but time taken to establish parameters of behaviour rarely proves to be lost time.

We know that we, as teachers, can too often suffer from the 'curse of the expert'. That is to say, we can overlook the nuanced behaviours that made us successful learners in our time at school.

Take the seemingly simple act of listening. We need to show students how to listen actively. Students need to understand the language of non-verbal communication: leaning in slightly, nodding, giving eye contact and asking questions for clarification, etc. It is a series of implicit behaviours that we need to make explicit.

Simple, shorthand statements matter for confident and clear behaviour management. With the listening described above, students can know exactly what you mean when you simply state 'active listening everybody'. They become the cornerstone of classroom routines and they curtail misbehaviour and shine a light on the behaviours we want and expect. When students learn how to truly listen the results can be revelatory, but simply explaining how to enact these behaviours we wish to see will not make it so.

Repetition of our message, and some dogged determination, is also required.

If you want great work from students you will need to inspire their trust, but we must also make clear that we expect that they dredge every improvement possible out of what they are doing before they can sit back in the glow of their excellent work. This requires making excellent work visible. Once visible, it takes a relentless pursuit of those standards. If work is unfinished, reject it. If work is hurried and even marginally substandard, then reject it.

No doubt it takes effort and time to establish your expectations (and no little organisation to request work to be repeated), but setting the bar high is essential.

Students play a clever game of making judgements. If your standard is higher than another teacher, then they will work harder for you. If they have multiple homework assignments, then they will do your homework first and with their best effort. Of course, the best of all possible worlds is that *every* teacher in the school is working hard at establishing the same standard of excellence, but we must start with our actions and our high expectations first.

The second move: Establish the rules

We come to the subject of much debate: school and classroom rules. Let's keep this simple. Rules do not crush the humanity and individuality of our students. Instead, they provide clear expectations for learning to thrive for everybody.

If you wish, share a dialogue with your students about which rules are the most significant, but don't for a moment think that having clear, no-nonsense rules is a negative act. Have rules, establish them early, and make them an integral part of lesson routines. I have spent the opening lesson of many a school year slowly going through the rules of my classroom.

Every week, these clear and concise messages – three or four should do it – are reiterated and made visible through explanation and example.

For me, respect and listening to others is paramount, as I have already stated. Learning flows from the spring of listening. I make respectful and active listening rule number one. I'll often elicit other rules from students, amazing them when my rules nearly exactly match their own. Common rules, like how to move about the classroom and how to respect others, may complete your personal repertoire.

Of course, one lesson does not establish excellent behaviour. That takes habit. I am in favour of a gradual approach. In the first few weeks, consciously note when individual rules are broken, making a not-so-subtle show of following up with sanctions. Sometimes I think most students are in on this charade, but it makes for a feeling of safety and certainty all the same.

By getting organised and establishing consistency in the first few months with our new classes, then we no doubt gain time and improve learning later on in the school year.[3]

The third move: Confidently manage the physical space of the room

Our behaviour management and our teaching begins before the lesson, given our reputation, but even that can be forgotten in the threshing waves of any given day for some of our students. They act on impulses that are too often beyond their conscious control.

Movement and tactical positioning around the classroom space becomes key in initiating your confident control, reminding the students of your status in the room. This is what is meant by the woolly term *presence*.

The opening of the lesson is clearly a crucial point for establishing your control. We can enact a series of small behaviours that convey assertiveness: greeting students at the door of the room with a relaxed smile, conveying preparedness and calm, primes your students for positive behaviour. Fumbling at the computer and searching frantically for your lesson resource sends the wrong message to your class.

The welcome into the classroom also allows you to make those crucial judgements about the mood of your students, settling and reassuring those students who need it. As we know, expert teachers know their students well and read their smallest of behaviours, responding flexibly when required.

Once they are in the classroom you can take up a central space in the room, conveying the confident call of 'this is my turf!' before then directing students to little jobs, quickly, with short, confident explanations:

- 'John – lined paper, one piece each – thanks.'
- 'Claire, can you lower the blinds a little.'
- 'Boys – bags. Move them under the desk – thank you.'

Too often we use conditional language: 'Could you please hand out the paper John?' or 'Would you mind listening please?' Although polite, using a tentative question, rather than a command, sends a small but significant message to our students that they could refuse your direction. You needn't forsake politeness: saying thank you can be positive without losing the power and clarity of a command. We can prove respectful, whilst making students subconsciously assume the behaviour you have directed is quite natural and appropriate.

We should err on the side of using commands and steer clear from tentative requests. If we couple our assertive commands with decisive gestures: pointing toward the paper tray, tapping on the bags to be moved, and more, we will then strike students as confident and authoritative. Once their confidence in us is established, we can choose to gradually ease off with our assertiveness.

Anticipating small acts of off-task behaviour, like chatting absent-mindedly, or talking whilst another student is giving an explanation, can often demand an all-seeing eye. We cannot hope for the head movement of an owl, so regularly moving around the room, anticipating and modifying how students behave, is essential. It can be done quietly and subtly if you position yourself in the eye-line of students, with a little nimble movement about the room.

A phantom pen tapper, or a hellish whistling pen, has foxed most teachers at one time or another. Listening intently, we can scan the class for clues of the furtive act. We shouldn't berate the class en masse. Instead, we can confidently manage our space. First, we move in the direction of the sound. We wait patiently. If we gain control and silence we can move on, but if the sound reappears, we can subtly speak to a narrow group of suspected students, warning them of repercussions and, if absolutely necessary, undertake a lengthy process to establish the root of the problem. If you have high standards and you are relentlessly consistent with them, they will invariably back down.

Expert teachers cut off the oxygen of misbehaviour at the source by managing the space in the room. They spy some stray eye contact when students should be working and they clench a furrowed brow to indicate their subtle command to refocus. For a student tapping away or humming a tune, the universal gesture of a finger pressed to the lips proves an unobtrusive and clear signal of confident control.

Expert teachers control the classroom space, creating their own consistent paths around the room. In his book, *Teach Like A Champion*, which is filled with useful tips for behaviour management, Doug Lemov suggests that teachers should have the confidence to 'break the plane'. That is to say, moving beyond that imaginary line a few feet from the front of the classroom, usually just in front of the first desks where the students sit to face the teacher. Too many teachers are pinned to the board at the front and others unwittingly retreat to the safe confines behind the teacher desk.

A crucial signal of physical confidence is passing that imaginary boundary to assert our physical influence.

Students quickly become used to your typical positional 'hotspots' around the room and they can commit to being more focused in the knowledge that you are constantly surveying how each student is doing.

A confident teacher's 'presence' can be distilled down to a series of such movements, small signals and gestures. I have experienced a remarkable range of gestures and signals, all understood by students through repeated practice, such as:

- Two hands held horizontally at chest height, lowered slowly [Instruction: lower the volume]
- An arm raised straight in the air [Instruction: be silent]
- Raised eyebrows [Instruction: think about your current behaviour!]

To convey confidence and presence, waving frantically like a distressed air traffic controller isn't going to cut it. We must emit calm and control when directing behaviour. When we convey physical equanimity, our students subconsciously feel safer and their behaviours can become more controlled. Being a teenager is a risky business and their brains are built for unthinking, boundary-shoving behaviour, but we can becalm them and set them more at ease.

The fourth move: Voice control

Expert behaviour management can prove near hidden – a silent treatment where students can continue to focus intently on what is being learnt. There are of course many occasions when you need to quell misbehaviour by speaking assertively.

Simple and clear commands are the order of the day for the confident teacher. Too often, I have suffered in silence when observing a teacher who is desperately shushing their group. Some teachers, visibly lacking in confidence, shush away like a Victorian steam train. Students, given the opportunity, will judge the vague shush in their general direction as not being directed at them. It proves little more than hot air.

Instead, we need to convey a short, sonorous instruction: 'James: quiet – now. Thank you'. When we pare down our language to the essentials like this it is both direct and is less likely to disrupt the flow of the lesson for others.

The tone and expression in our voice is vital in conveying our confidence. A handy reminder is to be frog-like in delivery. Green frogs frighten off potential rivals with a deep croak and, of course, the bigger the frog the deeper the croak. Only wily and small green frogs have learnt to deepen their voice to imitate their bigger peers too. The power of our voice is similarly available to every teacher.

Managing student behaviour

We should be wary of judging that such an approach favours only male teachers with a naturally deep voice. Female teachers can exercise the same subtle message to students by deepening their tone compared to their typical voice. It is about making minor, but important, adjustments to our voice that can have a significant impact upon how our words are received.

Teachers, to convey assurance, can gradually lower their volume as they explain – subtly making students listen with extra focus – whilst deepening the tone of voice. Consciously varying and deepening our tone of voice is the stuff of stage actors and expert teachers, but it can be learnt and we can covertly experiment with our students when we get the chance.

Remember Doug Lemov talked about the power of practice. Varying our voice for effect is ripe for such practice.

We each have our unique personal voice, but we should consider that when teaching we are using our 'stage' voice – our *act-of-utter-confidence* voice. Our teaching voice has greater range, more emotion, and it conveys more explicit emphasis than our 'normal' voice. I have been caught once or twice using my 'teacher voice' when annoyed with my partner. Though it clearly didn't work with her – perhaps the fact that she recognised the different tone and range in my voice is no bad thing...or not.

Teach Like a Champion once again proves instructive. It is important that whilst we expect to control our voice, lowering our volume and deepening our tone when appropriate, we need the full attention of every student. Lemov simplifies this down to the hook: *100 per cent.*

It is simple. Always expect one hundred per cent attention. If we ask for silence, to listen to a student give a response, we need one hundred per cent active listening. It is common sense personified, but sometimes common sense isn't so common.

Any allowance for a lesser standard of behaviour and students will commit it to memory (and not in a good way). To allow students to chat to others when a fellow student is speaking is for me a cardinal sin. If '100 per cent' is not established here, then we will be unlikely to establish the classroom climate where great learning happens.

Allowing a lowly murmur of chatter will wholly undermine your authority and lower expectations. When we are tired, our willpower strained by a hard week, the temptation is to marginally loosen our expectations. We can easily slump in our chairs, letting minor rule-breaking go. We must fight off this quite natural urge.

If our classroom rules and expectations are well honed, we can loosen control with comfort, but our safest judgement is to always retain one hundred per cent consistency.

The fifth move: Managing confrontation

A student who is out of control is the stuff of sleepless nights for teachers. No aspect of teaching can generate the degree of worry that out of control student behaviour creates. We need to act with assertive confidence when such an incident occurs.

I have faced this type of situation many times and have always attempted to best judge the situation with care and sensitivity.

I started this chapter with the story of Jessica. Too many times she approached my classroom visibly ready to explode. A split second judgement was required. Our face is the prime communicator of our emotion. Her face told a bleak story. Entering the classroom or not was a key decision. Would not paying attention help to disarm the anger, or did Jessica need time outside of the classroom to cool off? What do you do?

Given such a crisis, a series of physical responses are required to help diffuse the emotions of the angry child:

Managing student behaviour

- **Recognise our stress.** The natural reaction is to match the strain of our angry student with a defensive raising of our voice to be heard, or by naturally assuming a defensive posture, such as halting students by pointing directly at them. We must fight this physical urge and concentrate on speaking slowly, calmly, in an assured voice.
- **Assume a non-threatening body position.** First, we need to take care not to threaten the student by conveying aggression. We can assume a non-threatening stance, such as standing sideways and avoiding a direct face-to-face position.
- **Take care with eye contact.** Where eye contact typically establishes a relationship, in such an instance of anger and loss of control, taking care to look away and not stare can help.
- **Mirroring and calm gestures.** The minutiae of our body language is essential. Avoid pointing or clenched fists – signs of stress and challenge – and instead place your arms by your side, using open hand gestures if needed. A subtle mirroring of their body language can help ease their anxiety and diffuse potential confrontation.
- **Listen.** When a student is angry, unsurprisingly, they can find it hard to think rationally. We need to take care to verbalise that we are listening. Calmly replying, 'I understand what you mean', or paraphrasing what they are exclaiming in clearer terms, can show that you are ready and willing to listen. Often, we need to let students articulate their anger, but it does need guidance.
- **Identify and explain the problem.** Once we are talking to the student and they are offloading, we can assert our confident control by appraising the problem and explaining it to them clearly.
- **Assert our position with calm.** We need to explain how we feel about their behaviour, about the lesson ahead, and the other students who need our attention.

We can acknowledge what we want and what we don't want, before recognising their response.

- **Negotiate with care.** We can never concede ground that means our other students may have their learning compromised, but listening and negotiating the best settlement to see a solution ahead is required. The teen brain is programmed to revel in risk and not to consider the consequences. Sometimes a little time is all that is required, but at other times, calmly articulating and applying the familiar school sanctions proves essential.

Instances of erupting anger and discord are commonplace even in the best schools. They can be diffused or exacerbated in a matter of seconds. We can take a leaf out of the book of a doctor in this instance. A typical conversation with a patient, which can of course prove intensely private and distressing, can be just like an incident in school with a highly emotional student, so we can take care to deploy the *BATHE technique*. This applies to the approach we take to our interaction:

Background ('Tell me about what has happened in the lesson.')

Affect ('How do you feel about what happened and what was said?')

Trouble ('What is upsetting you most about what was said in the lesson?')

Handling ('How are you feeling about what X said to you in the lesson?')

Empathy ('That must have been really difficult for you...')

Such an event in the school day, showing empathy and soothing a distressed student, can prove our most important action. We need to approach it with a calm confidence.

Great group work

Group work is often conflated with poor student behaviour. Perhaps this is understandable given that, done badly, group work can prove a hotbed for misbehaviour. Conversely, done well, and given a tight structure, with clarity of roles and expectations, group work can prove a highly useful tool in the classroom.

The benefits of group talk are legion. They are shown in the development of crucial social skills, like empathy and seeing the viewpoints of others, accommodating them and developing our thinking. Well orchestrated, the knowledge of a group can outdo that of an individual, as the group aggregates and sifts through an array of ideas.

Opportunities for misbehaviour are naturally ingrained in the DNA of group work that is not well managed. 'Social loafing' is an all too common occurrence. When students are placed in a group they can take the opportunity to exert less effort, grabbing the chance to loaf, knowing their peers will make up for their slacking. Teachers can subsequently reward students unfairly, given one or more of the group have done all the work, whilst others were happy to coast along effortlessly.

Group work, quite naturally, can devolve into off-task chatter and impromptu social bonding on any topic that catches our students' interest. The benefits of cooperative small group work are too often outweighed by teachers lacking the confidence and skill to control and manage this learning method.

Indeed, such small group work is used relatively sparingly, with a recent study indicating less than 10 per cent of lesson time was spent doing group work.[4]

We should aim for a position where we are confident to deploy the right teaching strategy at the right time and not seeking to avoid any one approach for fear of it failing.

Thorough-going preparation for group work is a prerequisite for success and there are some sound principles for successful group work:

- **Establish the ground rules.** Once more, ensuring what we mean by communication – talk, listening, sharing and participating, etc – needs to be made visible to students, regardless of their age and stage. The few minutes invested in asking questions like, 'What do I mean by good collaboration?' are quickly regained when focused group discussion doesn't quickly dissolve into a meaningless debate about the best Marvel superhero.
- **Clear roles and goals.** Establishing clear roles, like researcher, summariser, note-taker, etc, all encourage focused discussion and learning, dissuading the temptation to loaf. What is really crucial is that there are group goals, but with individual responsibility.[5] One method is to have a group goal, such as producing code for a new school website in a computing class. Within that group goal though, there would be individual responsibilities that require each student to transfer important knowledge to one another, making them responsible for a distinct aspect of the task. By ensuring this reliance on one another, you can better eliminate loafing, thereby fairly balancing the workload in the group.
- **Precision timing.** We know we can all be downright awful at judging how long a task will take. For novice teachers, this is especially so. To ensure that behaviour is focused on the task, we need to share a dialogue about timing, giving markers along the way, without proving to be too much of a distraction.
- **Short, sharp stops.** Chatting and off-task behaviour is usually a product of waning interest and a lack of focus. It can happen with the most interesting of tasks, no

matter how well designed. It is important to judge the flow of the group working and stop at regular intervals. My experience indicates that students need refocusing (with an option for questions) every ten to fifteen minutes or so.

- **Monitoring.** Owning the classroom space and tactical positioning about the room throughout group work is essential. A confident teacher will recognise the subtle signs of loafing or chatting, before quickly asking short prompt questions, like, 'How are we progressing?' just to remind students of their role and responsibility. Sometimes groups will reach a genuine impasse that requires support. We must avoid learned helplessness, so asking them to reiterate the problem and talk through potential solutions, with short prompts, is a must.

With each group task we should be keenly aware of the subtle group dynamics at play. We know that the teen brain is thirsty to belong in their social group, so students often look to their important peers for validation and even consent. Each class has some 'key players' who set the tone in such group tasks. We must have a sharp understanding of the hierarchy at play here and form the groups accordingly.

There is no doubt that our degree of confidence in leading the class and managing such scenarios sends explicit messages to those 'key players' who are in control of the group dynamics, which are subtly shared between students.

Keeping in the flow

As explored earlier in the book, the notion of 'flow', made popular by Mihaly Csikszentmihalyi, describes a state of near complete immersion in a task. It captures that feeling when you are quite literally loving learning: you are getting useful feedback and you are finding your way. It might be best captured in that treasured moment when your student says, 'Is the lesson over already? That was quick!' Indeed, time seems to fly when you are in full 'flow'.

Confident behaviour management is about creating the conditions for this 'flow' to happen. It requires challenging work that pushes students without seeing them flailing; it takes timely feedback and a sensitive observation of the learning in the room; it takes trust in the teacher for our students to let go of their psychological barriers and anxieties, so that they can get stuck into challenging tasks.

This 'flow' is so crucial because it correlates with students maximising their time on task. By creating routine behaviours to maintain 'flow', we achieve a thousand marginal gains of time throughout the school year. Therefore a teacher with excellent behaviour management is more likely to see significant improvements in students' learning over the longer term.

Teachers know it when we see it, but it pays for us to talk about it and to best characterise what it looks like and sounds like in our own school context.

Take a moment to consider the last time you had a class in full flow. What was the activity and what were the strategies that you used to maintain such learning? If we can break it down into a pattern of moves, then we can seek to replicate it more often.

Seeing our students rise to the challenge and exhibit passion and pride in their work is what forges good relationships and great learning. It is what we go to school for. We can see, feel and feed off such responses from even the most challenging of students. That feeling we experience can in turn deepen our sense of commitment and hope, and it can sustain our confidence.

IN SHORT...

- We know that thinking and feeling are bound together to form our behaviours. Knowing our students and developing a trusting relationship is paramount for us to become truly confident in our behaviour management skills.
- A classroom climate characterised by focus and high effort is synonymous with successful learning. It requires clear and consistent parameters of behaviour being established. If a student is late, we relentlessly deal with that lateness; if there is a school-wide behaviour policy, we follow that policy with rigour (if there isn't, then we pursue our own as best we can).
- There are behaviour hotspots: the starts of lessons, transitions between tasks, and the ends of lessons are where misbehaviour most commonly flourishes. We need to take physical control of the classroom space at all times, but particularly at these points in our lessons.
- Expert behaviour management can appear somewhat invisible, but momentary gestures and shorthand instructions can characterise clarity, consistency and control.
- Confident teachers sweat the small stuff so that big behaviour incidents almost never develop. It looks quick and easy, but it takes a great deal of effort and expertise.
- We know that our confidence to manage poor behaviour and challenging classes is paramount for our students' success and for our well-being as teachers.

Notes

1   Kidd, C., Palmeri, H. and Aslin, R.N. (2013), 'Rational snacking: Young children's decision-making on the marshmallow task is moderated by beliefs about environmental reliability', *Cognition* 126: 109–114. [Online]. Available at: www.bcs.rochester.edu/people/aslin/pdfs/Kidd_Palmeri_Aslin_Cog2013.pdf (Accessed: 5 January 2015).
2   Zimmerman, B.J. (2000), 'Self-efficacy: An essential motive to learn', *Contemporary Educational Psychology*, 25: 82–91.
3   Cameron, C.E, McDonald Connor, C. and Morrison, F.J. (2005), 'Effects of variation in teacher organization on classroom functioning', *Journal of School Psychology*, 43 (1): 61–85.
4   Muijs, D. and Reynolds, D. (2011) *Effective Teaching: Evidence and Practice (3rd Edition)*, p 65. London: Sage Publications.
5   Slavin, R.E. (1995), *Co-operative Learning: Theory, Research and Practice (2nd Edition)*, Boston: Allyn and Bacon.

Chapter 2

Why do some children behave and some do not?

Introduction

Close your eyes and imagine the perfect class. Every child is working on activities they are clearly enjoying. There is a buzz in the atmosphere. It is one of enthusiasm and industry. Children share ideas, discuss their learning and know what they are trying to achieve. They have talked about the work together as a class and the teacher has helped them identify the criteria for the tasks. They will know they have achieved the desired outcome and the teacher will evaluate it to look for improvements. Every child is satisfied with their own progress because they do not view learning as a competition with their peers. To them it is a personal journey that will open up the world. One of the most prized aspects of this utopian class is the ability to ask questions. It is useful to imagine how you want things to be. Then it is simply a matter of working out how to achieve it.

The reality for many teachers is that there will be a mixed bag of children. Most will be good but there will be a number who could be challenging. The teacher will have to solve countless little problems, difficulties and disagreements. They will have to answer lots of questions about the work: what happened the day before, what's happening tomorrow, what's happening in the world and why is so-and-so doing this or that? With so much going on and so many demands it is not surprising that it does not always go right even for the most experienced.

Children do not set out to be naughty. Most are intrinsically good and want to please, but they all have the potential to stray. We

75

need to try to understand what prompts some children to misbehave so that we can respond in ways that will avoid conflicts and help them to improve. There is no mystery about how this can be achieved, it is simply a case of planning what you will do in different circumstances and adopting strategies that prevent spontaneous and irrational responses that inevitably result in emotionally charged, negative reactions.

In this chapter we will look at why children misbehave from three perspectives:

■ the position of the pupil;

■ the family context;

■ the school's influence.

We will then consider the notion of special needs and how requirements for individual children can best be met.

■ The pupils

An individual child may have specific clinical reasons that affect their behaviour. These include:

■ blindness or partial sight;

■ deafness or difficulty hearing;

■ speech difficulties;

■ mobility difficulties.

In the past, children with these difficulties were described as 'handicapped' or disabled and would usually have been educated in special schools. With the advent of a more open, inclusive attitude they are much more likely to receive their education in mainstream schools. Governments have required schools to make provision for these pupils. Consequently, changes have been made to the physical structures of the buildings to ensure the children have access. There are also many technical aids available including personal microphones connected to hearing aids, concept keyboards and speech-creating computers. Teachers and support staff can be trained in the use of sign language and Braille versions of a wide range of books can be obtained.

There are other clinical conditions that affect behaviour and educationalists are becoming far more aware of them.

Attention disorders

There are a number of these. Perhaps the most well known is Attention Deficit Hyperactivity Disorder and it can become a huge barrier to learning for a child and also the others in the class. The main feature is the child's inability to concentrate on an activity for an extended period of time. It is most common in boys and can be transmitted genetically. A third of all fathers who had ADHD have children with it. Once diagnosed, a child may be placed on medication, which is designed to help them concentrate in school. However, the problem is not often diagnosed until the child is well into their primary education. The signs to look for include many but not all of the following:

- difficulty in concentrating or focusing on-tasks and being easily distracted;

- low self-esteem because peers get fed up with his behaviour;

- overactive, fidgets or squirms;

- difficulty taking turns;

- blurting out answers to questions;

- difficulty following instructions;

- noisy when playing;

- talking excessively;

- often interrupts;

- loses things;

- engages in dangerous behaviour.

Strategies for dealing with children with ADHD

■ Make sure tasks are short. The ideal length is the age of the child plus two minutes for a normal child, e.g. eight years = ten minutes. For a child with ADHD this should be shorter. Limit most tasks to around five minutes.

■ Reward the child for staying on-task and completing it.

■ Explain the task carefully and make sure the child understands what to do. It may be useful to break up a five-minute task into three steps and give the instructions separately, e.g. Step 1 give instructions – then complete the work, Step 2 give instructions then complete the work.

■ ADHD children are often kinaesthetic learners so give them appropriate activities to help them channel their energy constructively.

■ Pair the child up with another responsible pupil and ask them to help in keeping the child on-task.

■ Watch out for the signs and intervene when you see the child going off-task.

■ Provide time-management support. Help the child to watch a clock so they will get an idea of how long common activities usually last.

■ Avoid copying-out activities as ADHD children do not write quickly or accurately.

■ Help the child keep the table tidy and organised.

■ Set up a personal checklist for the day.

■ Build movement into the lesson. For example, the child could come and show you how much they have done every ten minutes.

■ Find alternative consequences to detention at break to enable the child to get physical exercise and a change of scenery.

Hyperactivity

This is a medical condition that may possibly be aggravated by things like food, drink and additives. Much has already been written about potential links with certain foods with chemical additives and the changes they apparently bring about in behaviour. You may have drawn your own conclusions from observing children after they have had particular foods for lunch.

The strategies used to help a child with ADHD will be effective for children with a tendency to be hyperactive. It is also worth mentioning the food and drink that your class consume at breaks and lunchtimes. Work can be done in Science and PSHE as part of the Healthy Schools Programme on the benefits of a balanced diet and exercise. Classes and school councils can take a role in developing whole-school exercise programmes and menus for dinners. They can also be involved in discussions around the contents of a healthy packed lunch, tuck shops and the availability of fresh water and milk.

Autism and Asperger's Syndrome

Children with autism can exhibit behaviour that ranges from being barely noticeable to the extreme where they seem distant and unreachable. When it is that severe they are described as being in a world of their own. The milder form of autism, known as Asperger's Syndrome, is the more common in mainstream schools. A child with this condition may exhibit any number of the following characteristics:

- fixed in their ways and very dogmatic;

- gaze avoidance – does not make eye contact;

- socially inept;

- unaware of the way conversation is developing, resulting in unrelated comments and interruptions;

- physically weak with poor coordination;

- unexplainable outbursts of anger;

- unable to deal with changes in routines;

- fussy eater;

- has to wear specific items of clothing and certain colours;

- cannot tolerate certain sounds, loud noise, colours, smells;

- reading may be advanced but abstract comprehension is absent;

- evidence of creativity in sophisticated work but this may actually be extremely accurate replication of things remembered, e.g. well-drawn, detailed pictures of buildings;

- photographic memory;

- phenomenal ability to calculate, e.g. can compute quickly or provide days and dates for exact years.

Autism can vary and is described as a spectrum. Children cannot be easily diagnosed and so caution should be taken not to assume that they are autistic simply because they present with some of these behaviours.

Strategies for dealing with children with Asperger's Syndrome

Children who have either been diagnosed with Asperger's Syndrome or are showing some of the behaviours described earlier can be helped using a range of strategies. It is unlikely that you will be able to change their behaviour or responses but you will be able to help them be more included in what the whole class do if you adapt around their needs. There is a wide variety of strategies so only a selection is listed here.

- Provide a timetable of the day's events including activities not shown on the curriculum timetable.

- Alert the child as soon as possible of any potential staff changes or activities.

- Signal the end of activities, tasks, lessons, etc. five minutes before they actually end so the child knows they must finish what they are doing.

- Do not challenge the child in the same way as you would when other children misbehave. Do not insist they look at you when you are talking to them. If they are doing something different to what you asked or expected, talk to them about it. Autistic children will interpret instructions literally. Their actions may appear to be deliberate acts of mischief or cheekiness but in fact they are alternative ways of doing things. For example, if the teacher asks the class to write something under the title, an autistic child may turn to the next page and write it on the top line so it is literally under the title (on the other side of the sheet).

- Do not pressure the child to take all the food at lunch. They may feel they can eat only certain things or be unable to tolerate having certain foods like baked beans touching the fish. The child will not starve or go hungry so it is better not to get into a conflict over it.

- Work may be untidy or some activities done in an unsatisfactory way such as PE or swimming. The child may lack the coordination to do them any better so see their efforts for what they are.

- Provide a safe haven for the child during playtimes. Allow them to come off the playground if things get difficult. Children with Asperger's are possible targets for bullying.

- Social stories can be used to help them work through various problems that we would solve by being aware of the signs and feelings of others.

Tourette's Syndrome

This is a relatively rare disorder of movement named after the French neurologist Gilles de la Tourette who first described it in 1885. It begins in childhood with repetitive tics and facial grimaces. Involuntary grunts and other noises may start as the disease takes hold. In around 50% of cases, the sufferer has episodes of foul language.

It is more common in males and often undiagnosed because of its strange symptoms. It is a life-long condition but can be helped with medication. Many children at primary school may exhibit nervous tics and movement difficulties that are not Tourette's Syndrome. However, a child presenting with many of these symptoms may be in the early stages of the disease.

Non-clinical reasons for poor behaviour

There are many reasons why a child may not behave appropriately. Serious misbehaviour is a cry for help. The child is anxious and stressed and is not able to talk about their worries so they seek attention in other ways.

Poor self-esteem

This can be associated with many of the clinical conditions described earlier but it is also a common factor in many of the children who have difficulties with their behaviour at school. There are some children who have a personality trait that prevents them from coping with the attention they encounter. They are shy and do not like being put on the spot and in the public eye. When a teacher asks them a question or praises them in front of the whole class they go into meltdown because they are so embarrassed. They will not misbehave in a defiant way but their response may seem like non-compliance.

Then there are the children who do not get a return on their studies and see themselves as 'thick'. They are no good at sport and do not excel at any other hobbies or activities. They try to gain respect in order to boost their self-image by being a class clown or a bully. They are victims of a system that compares one pupil with another. Rendall and Stuart (2005) argue that there are a number of domains to self-esteem. A child may have a good self-image in some domains of their life such as among peers, with their family or of relationships or activities like sport. It is in the school-based domains of academic work that low self-esteem and poor self-image are most likely to occur.

The 'boundary tester'

Some children develop an urge to test the teacher to find out how far they can push the boundaries. There may be a legitimate reason for doing this. It could be that the child is very insecure and needs to know that the teacher has strong boundaries that will provide security. There are children who want the opposite: they want to know how much freedom they are allowed. They will go to the wire and beyond to see what happens. A firm response will probably end further testing, as they will learn where the boundary is.

Poor motivation

You cannot please all the people all of the time. There will be occasions when a child is bored. You may try everything you can think of to make the work fun and engaging but the task, the subject or school itself does not seem to interest the child on a particular day. The result will be that they disengage and look for their own ways to alleviate their boredom. This is when the trouble occurs.

Peer pressure

Young children in a school setting suddenly find themselves outside the safety and security of the family home. They are independent from their parents and face a new, daunting challenge of the classroom with its rules and competition for attention of other pupils. The sense of being alone and unsure of things motivates many children to align themselves with the peer group. They are looking for normality and a feeling of belonging that they get when they become part of a group.

Hierarchies develop in classrooms and children become subjected to the pressure of the peer group. It can be a positive force but it also has its negative side when individual members of the group get coerced into doing foolish things. This can lead to bullying and abuse if it goes unchecked. Peer pressure can be powerful and can transcend the authority of the teacher, the school and even the parents.

Rifts and rivalries

Children can be the best of friends one minute and then total enemies the next. Arguments and conflicts can occur for what would seem to be the most trivial of reasons. Disagreements develop because of possessions, games or who is in or out of a friendship group. Feuds break out and cause rifts that can lead to quite serious fights that you will have to deal with. Knowing what is going on in the class is important if you are to maintain order and keep the peace.

A potential area of conflict is the arrival of a new pupil. They may challenge the existing hierarchy and upset the equilibrium. One way of preventing this is to have a class order and any newcomer is placed at the end, at least for the first term. This reduces the likelihood of any jostling for power because stability is achieved when everyone knows and accepts their place.

No self-control

A lot of silly behaviour in young children is due to their lack of self-control and not deliberate defiance, as some teachers would believe. They have not fully developed their social awareness and when they find themselves in certain situations they do not know how to behave properly. Changes in routine, meeting new people, moving rooms or getting brand new equipment can trigger excitable behaviour. It may be a way of concealing the nervousness they feel. The significant message of this book is to acquire the strategies to help children develop their self-control.

The 'out there' culture

It is very common for children involved in incidents to see themselves as victims. They look to blame others for things that they were involved in. They do not accept responsibility for their own behaviour. The key strategy promoted in this book is to get children to take that responsibility. This is achieved by helping them understand how their actions can have an impact on the outcome and making them aware of their choices. There are many new resources available in schools including the National Primary Strategy 'Social and Emotional Aspects of Learning' pack (2005). The purpose behind the activities in the pack is to help children consider questions like 'What did I do?', 'What choices do I have?', 'How do I feel about . . . ?' and 'How will it affect others?' The resources can be used in assemblies, circle time, PSHE and curriculum lessons.

■ **The family**

The family dynamics and the home can be a major factor in determining a child's behaviour. The level of stability and the parents' attitudes towards their children must have an influence.

The critical incident

Children who do not have a clinical reason for their behavioural difficulties must have another cause that triggers them. Significant numbers of troubled children appear to have experienced some kind of critical incident. The sorts of trauma likely to be at the root of their problems might include:

- parents divorcing;

- witnessing parents arguing or fighting;

- parent addiction to alcohol or drugs;

- parental depression;

- disowned or neglected by a parent;

- redundancy or long-term unemployment of a parent;

- witnessing abuse or being abused;

- family member going through a serious illness;

- bullied at home or in school;

- involvement in crime or drugs;

- family member convicted of a crime or in prison;

- refugee from a war zone.

The *Framework for the Assessment of Children in Need and their Families* (Department of Health 2000) provides a useful starting point for considering the triggers for challenging behaviour (see Figure 2.1).

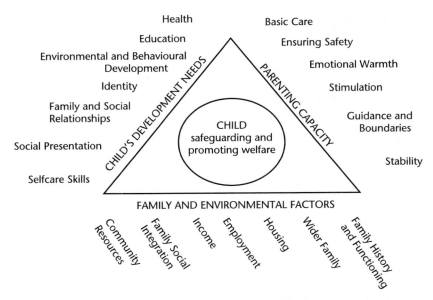

Figure 2.1 Assessment framework (Source: Department of Health 2000)

Exactly how such traumatic events lead to poor behaviour is not the subject of this book, but it would seem that there is more than a coincidental link.

Poor levels of care

The mental and physical well-being of the young dependant is the responsibility of the parent/carer. Inadequate levels of care lead to problems in the physical and cognitive development of the child and their behaviour. It is not uncommon for some children to come to school without having had any breakfast. They may be dishevelled, dirty and even have nits. Their home life is probably quite chaotic and there may be many reasons why their parents do not care for them adequately. However, that does not stop these children from feeling hungry or being uncomfortable in their dirty clothes. They may not be able to explain why they are unsettled but their behaviour usually reflects their feelings.

Parents who send their children to school with poorly prepared packed lunches will be inadvertently contributing to classroom problems. Processed foods are convenient and easily obtainable but may well be of low nutritional value. They contain high levels of additives which some believe contributes to hyperactivity in young children. Then there are children with very little in their lunch boxes. They have barely enough calories to see them through the day and what they do have is of poor quality. Staff who discover children with inadequate amounts of food usually manage to conjure up something extra to help, but longer-term solutions are required. The opposite to this are the over-fed children who eat far too much and do insufficient exercise. They spend long periods of time sitting down watching television or playing computer games. In the end their weight becomes a barrier and they find they cannot do active things. Children who get into this situation become targets for bullying because they are different from the rest.

Abuse and neglect

In tragic cases, poor care develops into serious neglect. This may occur when the parent/carer has suffered a critical incident such as the death of a loved one, a serious illness or a separation, any of which may be accompanied by depression and an over-use of drugs or alcohol. The signs become noticeable in the child. At its worst they lack energy, are unwashed and exhibit sudden changes in behaviour. There may be marks on their bodies and unexplained absences.

Children taken into care after being badly abused will not immediately change and behave normally again. Sometimes their experiences are so traumatic that they cause serious psychological effects and they need professional help.

Very aggressive and challenging children are likely to be frightened and anxious. They may have lost control of many aspects of their life and feel helpless. They search around for things they can control such as school and their peers, which eventually leads to aggressive acts.

The school and the teachers

We can have little impact on what happens at home. However, children are at school for six hours a day, five days a week, for thirty-nine weeks of the year. This is a significant amount of time to modify any inappropriate behaviour.

The question that needs consideration is whether school, as an experience for young people, is also a cause of poor behaviour. There are many incidents in school but they do not all involve children with troubled backgrounds. Children are often required to sit for long periods in crowded, uncomfortable conditions, performing written tasks and furnishing the answers to countless questions. Given the numbers of children involved, it is not surprising that they misbehave. Obviously, children with clinical conditions or complicated home lives have the potential to contribute to the problems, but the role of the teacher cannot be ruled out.

When the Labour Government took office in 1997 it placed education at the heart of its reforms. A great deal of emphasis was put on raising achievement and this produced significant tensions between schools, local authorities and the Government itself. Measurable outcomes were prioritised in the form of results and targets in the push to improve standards in state schools. Parsons (1999) describes a continuum that schools can be positioned on that ranges from a social, democratic and humanist approach through to a controlling one. Schools that prioritise values such as high academic standards, a traditional curriculum and a controlled school population tend to be less tolerant of difference and expect conformity. Rendall and Stuart (2005) argue that such schools give

> *a lower priority to the pastoral role including the opportunity to address individual children's strengths in areas other than the traditional subjects.*

The unspoken expectation is that a teacher should be able to control their class. However, the degree of preparation that teachers get for this can vary, which leads to the development of many different approaches.

The variations in styles of behaviour management, coupled with variations in ethos, give rise to significant ambiguity and even confusion among staff and children about what is required. Caulby and Harper (1985) argue that the way a school is organised can affect pupil behaviour. In particular, they link it to the school ethos. The way the staff approach the management of behaviour can determine the level of misbehaviour and can even be a significant cause of it. The following pages briefly describe some of the factors concerning us as teachers that can affect the way children behave in our classes.

Inconsistency and unfairness

Many children develop very strong moral values including a good sense of what is right and wrong. They are able to spot inconsistencies and expect them to be addressed. When an inconsistency occurs children perceive it as an injustice. A good example of this is when a class are told to line up quietly and a child messes around. The teacher spots it but does not give the child a consequence. A few minutes later another child does the same thing and the teacher loses her patience. She gets more cross with the second child, tells them she is fed up with being ignored and gives them a detention. This inconsistent approach is clearly unfair.

The self-fulfilling prophecy

We make judgements about people within seconds of meeting them. First impressions are based upon a complex set of assessments of the visual signs we receive. As teachers, we may be told about a particular child or class prior to taking them. This information can be useful because it allows us to consider how we can best serve the children we teach. It may also have a detrimental effect. We may be told that a child has been poorly behaved, which prejudices our view before we have even met them.

Children will respond to us and the ways we treat them. Talking up a class or an individual child will make them feel good and start to believe in themselves. Conversely, using negative comments and phrases like 'You are always the one who starts it . . .' or 'I might have known it would be you who was to blame' will be demotivating and the child may eventually just give up. They will feel they can never do anything right in your eyes and become what you are labelling them. It is important to keep an open mind and approach every child positively by building in strategies to help them change rather than write them off.

Being confrontational

One style that some teachers adopt is to be oppressive. They believe that they are in charge and the children should not challenge their authority. When a child does, they are dealt with in a confrontational and often aggressive way. The effect on the child is to either frighten them into submission or provoke them into defiance. Either way brings no real advantages, only difficulties (see Chapter 1: How do children learn?). Confrontation is not a solution and is a barrier in the development of a positive, calm climate that is conducive to learning.

Weak responses

The opposite to the aggressive style is the passive response. The teacher will try to persuade pupils to follow directions and they will detect a weakness of character and exploit it. The passive teacher will fail to show they are the leader in the classroom and the result will be unruly children doing their own thing. Weak responses to incidents leave an uncertain void. Children expect adults to take control to resolve problems. They do not expect a lack of response.

Sour or bad-tempered moments

Everybody has their off-days and teachers are no exception. We need to guard against our emotions taking control during these times. That is why a well-thought-through behaviour plan is essential. It will enable you to use procedures to manage difficult situations when you are at a low point.

What is totally unacceptable is a teacher who seems to be permanently sour. Teachers who get to this state are jeopardising the education of their pupils. The joy of teaching seems to have disappeared for them and they should review their future because many children regard their lessons as downright awful. Such teachers have little respect for the pupils and set a poor example by being rude and bad tempered. They seem unapproachable and engender a climate of distrust in their classroom.

Delivery of lessons

One obvious source of behaviour problems can be the lesson and the quality of the teaching. A good lesson with appropriate activities can enthuse and inspire. A poorly thought-through lesson with activities that do not match the abilities of the pupils can switch them off.

Being a teacher is very demanding in many ways. To teach successfully requires a wide repertoire of skills. We should be secure in our knowledge of the subjects and how to teach each one. We need to know what each pupil is capable of and how they can be challenged. The activities should be varied to enable children with different learning styles to benefit. The delivery of the lesson must connect what has been learned with what comes next so that the class know where they are going. The teacher should activate their minds so they can take on new ideas and then demonstrate the application of them in a variety of contexts. Finally, the learning should be consolidated so that the children can recognise what they have learned and what they personally feel they need to do next (see Chapter 1: How do children learn?). Careful structuring of the learning taking all this into consideration is a complex and time-consuming task but it can yield surprising results.

Things do not always go smoothly and some teachers have difficulty working out how to teach some subjects, which can lead to ineffective lessons. This is not a failing. What is inexcusable is the failure to review why a lesson did not go well and then try to make improvements. Many teachers do this as a matter of course. You can usually tell when things have not gone well and your pupils will also give you some indication. Keeping the learning personal and alive for the children will minimise behaviour problems.

Low expectations

Classes of pupils are not homogeneous groups – there will be a spread of abilities. In many comprehensive schools this is likely to be quite wide, especially if there is a high proportion of children with learning difficulties. You could find you have the full ability range from Reception to Level 5. This is a daunting prospect because the planning of suitable activities to meet individual needs becomes a complicated task. Yet it can be achieved by organising the pupils into four groups: high, average, low ability and those with special needs who would benefit from being in a group of their own. Group composition will vary with subjects and should be organised using assessment data and individual education plans that you have. Current thinking also includes a 'wave' approach. Wave 1 – pupils who can make expected progress in the lesson. Wave 2 – pupils who could make progress if they were placed in groups with support. Wave 3 – pupils who are significantly delayed in their learning and need intensive support, possibly outside of some lessons.

Children are able to tell when a teacher has low expectations. They find the activities prosaic and easy, resulting in early completion. They soon realise they can get by with very little effort. Then the problems start because they have nothing to do. The unstructured time leads to behaviour issues. It is at those times that the teacher is under pressure because the children will distract those who are still working. Time invested in planning how to challenge the more able will reap dividends. The pupils will remain engaged and on-task, leaving you free to concentrate on managing the learning of all the pupils rather than helping some and dealing with the incidents of others.

Personalise the learning

Linking the learning to the personal experiences of the pupils will motivate them to engage more readily with it. Putting the idea or concept into a context will help the children understand why they are studying it. This can be quite difficult with some subjects, especially if the topic is an abstract one.

A very effective way of personalising something is to ask the children to empathise or role-play. Proposing questions like 'How would you feel if . . . ?', 'What would you do . . . ?', 'Can you think of another way that they could . . . ?' will bring the learning alive and let the pupils respond to it rather than treating them as empty vessels to be filled with facts.

We owe it to the pupils to look for ways that will help them get interested in the work, otherwise they will just switch off and cause trouble.

Boundaries

Children need boundaries to help them learn how to behave in different contexts. Problems can occur when the boundaries are absent or poorly defined. Teachers who have clear rules that are simple to follow and upheld in a fair and consistent way minimise problems.

Rules are put in place to protect the rights and feelings of the community. It is the responsibility of everyone to ensure they are adhered to (see Chapter 6: Values, beliefs and expectations). The adults in schools have a duty to establish the rules and children expect them to do this. Demonstrating that you are the leader and adult in the room is an essential part of ensuring that the children will behave. Once they know you are in charge they can relax and feel secure. Teachers who are not assertive and fail to establish a system of good order could end up with a troublesome class. The same can apply in the home. Parents who do not demonstrate their position allow their children to push back the boundaries and, ultimately, take control.

Seating

The way children are seated in a classroom can lead to problems. Allowing them to sit where they want will lead to small pockets of children who may have a tendency to be distracted. The solution is to work out a seating plan in advance. This requires knowledge of the friendship groups and the children who are likely to misbehave so that you can seat them appropriately. Some teachers favour a boy–girl arrangement but this can be uncomfortable for shy pupils.

There may be children in the group who have problems with their eyesight or hearing and need to be near the front. It may not be apparent at first but if you find a child is beginning to misbehave and/or their work is below standard, it is worth finding out whether this could be the reason.

Special needs

There are occasions when a class has a higher proportion of children with special needs. This is more likely in one-form-entry schools. It may be that they get identified only once they have been at the school for a number of years. Whatever the reason, it can be quite a challenge for a teacher and the behaviour of the class could be affected, leading to serious problems. If you find you are in this position you should discuss it with the Special Educational Needs Coordinator (SENCO) to decide how best to use the support. Make sure you have a clear behaviour code to ensure children understand what is expected of them.

Absence

The nature of planning curriculum subjects results in mini-programmes of work that focus on topics or key concepts. These may span a whole week for core subjects or a number of weeks for foundation subjects. Children who are absent could miss important lessons where new concepts are introduced. Then they find they do not understand what they are doing and fall behind everyone else. The teacher will endeavour to help the child but it is always harder to do once the rest of the class have moved on.

Children who are absent for short periods on a regular basis will experience this difficulty more often and it can create behavioural problems. Their feelings of being left out or in need of special attention single them out. They may resent the need for individual help or find they are waiting around for it and then get bored. Whatever the reason, the likelihood of an incident is increased, so teachers in this position need to take steps to avoid it.

Bullying

This is probably one of the darker sources of poor behaviour. It can be very difficult to detect and is often concealed by both the victim and the perpetrator. Behaviour that is out of keeping may be a sign that bullying is going on. A child may try to fit in with a particular peer group by doing things to impress them or copying their behaviour. Alternatively, a child being bullied may misbehave, either unwittingly or deliberately, to draw attention to themselves as a cry for help.

Bullying usually occurs when an individual or a group feel they are powerful and can force others to submit to them. It comes in many forms. It can be physical, verbal or territorial in the sense that the group isolates the victim and prevents them entering their circle or gang. Victims generally have something that singles them out as different. It may be a physical feature or an aspect of their personality. A child may have a need, such as wanting to be friends or to have someone to share their interests. The bully picks up on that need and exploits it. Children with learning difficulties are susceptible to being bullied because they are noticeable in schools by the support they get and the different work they may do.

All schools have their own ways of dealing with bullying, which can vary from sweeping it under the carpet and denying it is happening to some sophisticated approaches that include face-to-face interviews, restorative justice and strict contracts for change. The teacher's role is to be vigilant for the signs and act early when they think it is going on. Poor self-esteem is often at the root of bullying and can result in a child becoming vulnerable and a victim of bullying or even needing to bully others.

Redefining special needs

Rendall and Stuart (2005) suggest that special needs are not solely located within the child. They argue that there is a set of interrelated

95

conditions involved which are located within the family and the school as well as the child. This view is very similar in many ways to the *Framework for the Assessment of Children in Need and their Families* mentioned earlier in this chapter.

All children have learning needs. The school system is set up in a way that allows the majority (those who could be described as having normal intellectual and physical development) to have their needs catered for through the curriculum designed for their year group. There are expected year group targets available from the Department for Education and Skills (DfES) on the Standards website (www.dfes.gov.uk). These clearly identify what children should be able to do in each subject by the end of any academic year. There will usually be a group of children who exceed these expectations in one or more subjects and who are described as 'gifted' or 'talented'. There will also be a group who do not reach the targets for their age in one or more subjects. A child who falls well below the expected levels in the core subjects is described as having special needs. In some cases the need is so profound that they have an educational statement. This is a legal document that details the strategies and the support the child is entitled to receive to enable them to meet the targets specified in it.

Identifying a need in an individual prompts a number of new questions. Does the child have difficulty in their learning that can be attributed to their cognitive development? Is it due to family circumstances or the strategies the school is using? When a child is underperforming, we need to interrogate what we do. We should consider whether changes could be made that might help. For example, if a child had behavioural difficulties and we changed our responses from rules and direct instructions to choices, would things be different?

We try to help pupils do their best by fostering a positive climate for learning and putting in place more opportunities for them to take responsibility for their own behaviour. In the next chapter, we will consider how the style you adopt as a teacher can obstruct or advance you towards this goal.

■ Review

Pupils may have a range of clinical reasons that will cause them to behave inappropriately.

NON-CLINICAL REASONS SUCH AS POOR SELF-ESTEEM, LACK OF BOUNDARIES OR MOTIVATION, PEER PRESSURE AND AN ABSENCE OF SELF-CONTROL MAY PREVENT A CHILD BEHAVING WELL.

Children will often try to blame others and we need to help them to recognise that if they were involved, they were making a choice.

Family dynamics may be a major reason for behavioural difficulties.

Significant numbers of troubled children have experienced a serious critical incident in their past.

Schools can have an impact on inappropriate behaviour, both in its cause and with helping children to modify it.

A teacher's style can be a factor in causing a child to misbehave.

Special needs are not always located within the child. The family and even the school may have 'special needs' that affect the way a child behaves.

3.3 Managing classroom behaviour
Adopting a positive approach

Philip Garner

Introduction

This unit is designed to enable you to enhance your knowledge and skills in classroom management, and especially to support the development of positive approaches in dealing with pupil behaviour. It takes account of some of the most recent shifts in thinking and policy in this important dimension of your initial teacher education (ITE) programme. This includes advice that has emerged from a 'behaviour expert' nominated by the Department for Education (DfE), providing practical, hands-on information to teachers (DfE 2010a). More recently, this useful guidance has been reinforced (DfE 2014a: 6), with an emphasis that 'Teachers have statutory authority to discipline pupils whose behaviour is unacceptable, who break the school rules or who fail to follow a reasonable instruction'.

There has been a noticeable move away from reactive approaches to dealing with unwanted behaviour over the last 15 or more years. Such approaches were characterised by a preoccupation with 'discipline' being something that the teacher imposes on pupils (Robertson 1996). Instead, a greater awareness of 'behaviour for learning' has become apparent, which is consistent with the quest to develop inclusive schooling for all learners. Even so, it should be clearly understood that such an approach to pupil behaviour does not diminish the importance of clear and explicit classroom rules to govern pupil behaviour – and their consistent application. You need to ensure that pupils are under no illusions that, as class teacher, you are in control; it is, after all, what they expect of you!

A 'behaviour for learning' approach emphasises the teacher's role in creating an appropriate climate in which all pupils can learn effectively. It encourages you to link pupil behaviour with their learning via three interlinked relationships: how pupils think about themselves (their relationship with themselves); how they view their relationship with others (both teachers and fellow pupils); and how they perceive themselves as a learner, relative to the curriculum (their relationship with the learning they are undertaking). Recognition of the interplay between these three relationships is seen as the basis of a preventative approach. It also places importance on the role of the pupils themselves, in learning to manage their own behaviour.

Understanding this way of working remains an important facet of a teacher's role in managing pupil behaviour. The most recent advice has balanced this with a requirement that all teachers – and especially those newly qualified – understand some basic guidelines regarding the way in which the occurrence of unacceptable behaviour by pupils in a classroom can be minimised. Such behaviour has been a consistent cause of concern on the part of teachers themselves, educational professionals, parents and politicians for many decades; some aspects of these concerns are dealt with in the section dealing with 'policy context'.

Current approaches to 'behaviour' in ITE programmes reflect the shift in emphasis in the way that the issue is being tackled. The focus is on a middle ground between the earlier focus on 'control' and 'discipline' and a more recent holistic approach that focuses more upon linking behaviour with achievement.

This unit does not provide detailed accounts of individual behavioural needs or characteristics. There is now an extensive literature relating to the practical aspects of behaviour management, which is widely accessible elsewhere (see, for example, Dix 2007; Haydn 2008; www.behaviour2learn. co.uk). The unit concentrates on both the principles underpinning the links between pupil behaviour and the taught curriculum, as well as some of the important practical dimensions involved in effectively managing 'pupil discipline' in the classroom.

OBJECTIVES

At the end of this unit, you should be able to:

■ recognise the policy context for promoting pupil learning in classrooms;
■ interrogate a definition of the term 'unacceptable behaviour' and understand the significance of its underlying causes;
■ recognise the importance of the links between pupil behaviour and their curriculum learning;
■ understand the classroom implications of the current guidance to teachers regarding pupil behaviour;
■ develop positive approaches to unacceptable behaviour that are based on relationships with pupils.

Check the requirements for your ITE programme to see which relate to this unit.

The current context: official advice and guidance

There has been an increasing emphasis upon the inclusion of a greater diversity of learners in mainstream schools in the last 20 or so years (DfEE 1999; DfES 2001a, 2003a). The underpinning ideology of educational inclusion is that the educational needs of all pupils in schools should be met, irrespective of their level of achievement or the nature of their behaviour (Evans and Lunt 2002). Thus, you will encounter a wide range of learner needs in your first encounters in the classroom. Pupils who exhibit what have been termed social, emotional and behavioural difficulties (SEBD) will almost certainly be present, even though recent changes in the Special educational needs (SEN) code of practice (DfE 2014k) have resulted in this category of pupils being removed from the remit of SEN provision. Such pupils have traditionally represented as many as 20 per cent of all pupils who have SEN (DfE 2014c). The challenging behaviour of these pupils is usually accompanied by underachievement or a specific educational need. In consequence, they will most likely be supported by the special educational needs coordinator (SENCO), teaching assistants and by other key workers in the school.

SEBD is a term that has previously referred to a continuum of behaviours, from relatively minor behaviour problems to serious mental illness (DfE 1994b). In this unit, the focus is principally on pupil behaviours that are viewed as low-level unacceptable behaviours – in other words, not those towards the more serious end of the continuum. However, you may sometimes encounter pupils who present more challenging behaviours in your classroom, including some who may abuse drugs and other substances; pupils with mental health needs and pupils who experience behaviour-related syndromes, such as attention deficit hyperactivity disorder (ADHD) or autistic spectrum disorders (ASD). Many of these behaviours, including those that are sometimes intense and very challenging to teachers, can be more effectively managed if you build proactive, positive strategies into your teaching. There are also existing school strategies and support (including a key teacher or tutor) who is directly involved in dealing with these more extreme behaviours. In addition, in instances where such pupils are present, such support will frequently be available from a teaching assistant who will work with the pupil in your classroom.

An important feature of a school's promotion of a 'positive climate', as well as its response to unacceptable behaviour, is the 'whole school behaviour policy' (DfE 2011d, 2014a). Its importance is stressed in straightforward terms: 'It is vital that the behaviour policy is clear, that it is well understood by staff, parents and pupils, and that it is consistently applied' (DfE 2014a: 5–6). As a matter of course, you should make sure that you familiarise yourself with its content. The government sets out clear guidelines regarding its content (below), although you should also recognise that individual schools vary according to the behaviour routines and rules they put in place:

1   a consistent approach to behaviour management;
2   strong school leadership;
3   classroom management;
4   rewards and sanctions;
5   behaviour strategies and the teaching of good behaviour;
6   staff development and support;
7   pupil support systems;
8   liaison with parents and other agencies;
9   managing pupil transition;
10 organisation and facilities.

A whole-school behaviour policy provides some of the basic building blocks that you use to help establish a positive classroom 'climate'; this term refers to the character or 'feel' of your classroom, as experienced by all those who experience it – teachers, pupils and any classroom visitors. A major influence on this is the class teacher's own repertoire of knowledge, skills and understanding about pupil behaviour and classroom management. To assist you in acquiring these attributes, you may be assisted by lead behaviour teachers, tutors and other suitably experienced professionals who provide practical support in positively managing behaviour (DCSF 2008c). In addition, further support can be provided by teachers from other educational settings; for example, pupil referral units (PRUs), special schools for pupils experiencing SEBD, teaching assistants and local authority (LA) personnel who have a specific brief for work in SEBD (Walker 2004).

Some of the key policy documents relating to pupil behaviour have already been referenced in this unit; a full listing is provided in the further reading at the end of the unit. These advice and guidance documents in England aim, among other things, to help teachers to promote positive behaviour and to support them in tackling issues of low-level unacceptable behaviour. They point to the importance of providing creative and positive learning environments for all pupils. They also provide a framework that you can use in order to develop a set of rules and routines based on the development of a positive relationship between yourself and the pupils. This is the first step in helping to insulate pupils from those factors (discussed later in this unit), which might cause them to behave inappropriately and, in consequence, fail to thrive as learners.

One related aspect of pupil behaviour that requires special mention is bullying. Like other unacceptable behaviours, bullying varies in its type and intensity. The current guidance on bullying in schools, which you should become familiar with, is provided in *Preventing and Tackling Bullying: Advice for Headteachers Staff and Governing Bodies* (DfE 2014h).

Finally, you are reminded that the Office for Standards in Education (Ofsted) framework includes 'behaviour and safety' as one of its key criteria for inspections (Ofsted 2012b). As well as being intrinsic to becoming a successful classroom teacher, there is a statutory emphasis that behaviour is a feature of teaching that will be under continuing close scrutiny in England, and no doubt in other countries, in the years ahead.

What is unacceptable behaviour?

Recent national advice and guidance on behaviour management in England emphasises the development of appropriate, positive behaviour. This has been identified as bringing significant benefits for all pupils (Redpath and Harker 1999). The guidance invites teachers to be clear about what behaviour they want pupils to engage in, and to model this as part of their teaching.

However, the term 'behaviour' has traditionally been taken to mean unacceptable behaviour. The Elton Report (DES 1989a) refers to misbehaviour as 'behaviour which causes concern to teachers'. The term is one that can variously be replaced by a range of other expressions that teachers use to describe unwanted, unacceptable behaviour by pupils. Thus, disruptive, challenging, antisocial, off-task, unwanted, emotional and behavioural difficulties (EBD) and SEBD are terms that are widely used, according to the personal orientation of the teacher concerned and to the type of problem behaviour being described.

The term 'unacceptable behaviour', as with its companion descriptors (see above), is often used as a catch-all expression for pupil behaviours that span a continuum (DfE 1994b). The so-called EBD continuum ranges from low-level unacceptable behaviour at one end (such as talking out of turn, distracting others, occasionally arriving late in class) to more serious, sometimes acting out behaviour, at the other (such as non-attendance, verbal or physical aggression, wilful disobedience and bullying). This confusion was recognised by DfE (1994b), which described EBD as all those behaviours that comprise a continuum from 'normal though unacceptable' to mental illness; confusion rather than clarity over definitions seemed to increase when the term EBD subsequently incorporated social difficulties into the spectrum to become SEBD (DCSF 2008c).

A previous version of the *SEN Code of Practice* (DfES 2001b: 93) defined 'children and young people who demonstrate features of emotional and behavioural difficulties' as those who are 'withdrawn and isolated, disruptive and disturbing, hyperactive and lacking concentration'.

DESIRABLE BEHAVIOUR	UNDESIRABLE BEHAVIOUR
L1. Attentive/interested in schoolwork • attentive to teacher, not easily distracted • interest in most schoolwork/starts promptly on set tasks/motivated • seems to enjoy school	• verbal off-task behaviours • does not finish work/gives up easily • constantly needs reminders/low attention span • negative approach to school
L2. Good learning organisation • competent in individual learning • tidy work at reasonable pace • can organise learning tasks	• forgetful, copies or rushes work • inaccurate, messy and slow work • fails to meet deadlines, not prepared
L3. Effective communicator • good communication skills (peers/adults) • knows when it's appropriate to speak • uses non-verbal signals and voice range • communicates in 1:1 or group settings	• poor communication skills • inappropriate timing of communication • constantly talks • lack of use of non-verbal skills
L4. Works efficiently in a group • works collaboratively • turn-takes in communication/listens • takes responsibility within a group	• refuses to share • does not take turns
L5. Seeks help where necessary • seeks attention from teacher when required • works independently or in groups when not requiring help	• constantly seeking assistance • makes excessive and inappropriate demands • does not ask 'finding out' questions
C6. Behaves respectfully towards staff • cooperative and compliant • responds positively to instruction • does not aim verbal aggression at teacher • interacts politely with teacher • does not deliberately try to annoy or answer the teacher rudely	• responds negatively to instruction • talks back impertinently to teacher • aims verbal aggression, swears at teacher • deliberately interrupts to annoy
C7. Shows respect to other pupils • uses appropriate language; does not swear • treats others as equals • does not dominate, bully or intimidate	• verbal violence at other pupils • scornful, use of social aggression (e.g. 'pushing in') • teases and bullies • inappropriate sexual behaviour
C8. Seeks attention appropriately • does not attract inappropriate attention • does not play the fool or show off • no attention-seeking behaviour • does not verbally disrupt • does not physically disrupt	• hums, fidgets, disturbs others • throws things, climbs on things • calls out. eats, runs around the class • shouts and otherwise attention seeks • does dangerous things without thought

Figure 3.3.1 Desirable and undesirable behaviour

Source: Adapted from QCA (2001b)

Key: L = learning behaviour; C = conduct/behaviour; E = emotional behaviour

DESIRABLE BEHAVIOUR	UNDESIRABLE BEHAVIOUR

C9. Physically peaceable
- does not show physical aggression
- does not pick on others
- is not cruel or spiteful
- avoids getting into fights with others
- does not have temper tantrums

- fights, aims physical violence at others
- loses temper, throws things
- bullies and intimidates physically
- cruel/spiteful

C10. Respects property
- takes care of own and others' property
- does not engage in vandalism
- does not steal

- poor respect for property
- destroys own or others' things
- steals things

E11. Has empathy
- is tolerant and considerate
- tries to identify with feelings of others
- tries to offer comfort
- is not emotionally detached
- does not laugh when others are upset

- intolerant
- emotionally detached
- selfish
- no awareness of feelings of others

E12. Is socially aware
- understands social interactions of self and peers
- appropriate verbal/non-verbal contacts
- not socially isolated
- has peer-group friends; not a loner
- doesn't frequently daydream
- actively involved in classroom activity
- not aloof, passive or withdrawn

- inactive, daydreams, stares into space
- withdrawn or unresponsive
- does not participate in class activity
- few friends
- not accepted or well-liked
- shows bizarre behaviour
- stares blankly, listless

E13. Is happy
- smiles and laughs appropriately
- should be able to have fun
- generally cheerful; seldom upset
- not discontented, sulky, morose

- depressed, unhappy or discontented
- prone to emotional upset, tearful
- infers suicide
- serious, sad, self-harming

E14. Is confident
- not anxious
- unafraid to try new things
- not self-conscious, doesn't feel inferior
- willing to read aloud, answer questions in class
- participates in group discussion

- anxious, tense, tearful
- reticent, fears failure, feels inferior
- lacks self-esteem, cautious, shy
- does not take initiative

E15. Emotionally stable/self-controlled
- no mood swings
- good emotional resilience, recovers quickly from upset
- manages own feelings
- not easily flustered or frustrated
- delays gratification

- inappropriate emotional reactions
- does not recover quickly from upsets
- does not express feelings
- frequent mood changes; irritable
- over-reacts; does not accept punishment or praise
- does not delay gratification

Figure 3.3.1 continued

The definition also includes those who display 'immature social skills and those who present challenging behaviours arising from other complex special needs'.

One of the major difficulties in defining what inappropriate behaviour constitutes is that it varies according to the perception, tolerance threshold, experience and management approach of individual teachers. What might be an unacceptable behaviour in your own classroom may be viewed in another context, or by another (student) teacher, as quite normal. Alternatively, what you accept as normal may be seen as unacceptable in another context or by another (student) teacher. This leads to confusion in the mind of pupils, and to potential tension between individual teachers in a school or between a student teacher and tutor or other experienced teacher. So it is important to recognise that: (a) pupil behaviour is described explicitly in terms of observable actions; and (b) responses to it take full regard of a school's policy concerning behaviour and apply it with consistency. When you describe a pupil behaviour, you should always ensure that your definition is of the behaviour itself and not a description of the pupil as a whole. This avoids any likelihood of the pupil being labelled as a disruptive pupil or a problem pupil.

The Qualifications and Curriculum Authority (QCA 2001b) usefully identified 15 behaviours by which a pupil's emotional and behavioural development might be defined and assessed. These were divided into learning behaviours, conduct behaviours and emotional behaviours. Each group is subdivided into sets of criteria, depicting desirable and undesirable behaviours (see Figure 3.3.1). Now complete Task 3.3.1.

 Task 3.3.1 School policy on pupil behaviour

Familiarise yourself with your placement school's whole-school policy on behaviour and attendance. Discuss it with another student teacher who is placed in a different school. Consider both the similarities and differences in the two policies. What are the implications of the document for you as a student teacher, particularly in respect of classroom management?

Record your reflections in your professional development portfolio (PDP).

Identifying or defining unacceptable behaviour is important if you are going to develop strategies to deal with it in ways that promote learning. You need to describe exactly what any unwanted behaviour actually comprises in order to give a precise and objective description of what has occurred. Importantly, you need to describe the behaviour itself, not the pupil, otherwise there may be unwarranted negative labelling of the pupil. Task 3.3.2 helps you to develop a definition of unacceptable behaviour.

Scoping the causal factors

As Ayers and Prytys (2002: 38) noted, 'The way in which behaviour is conceptualised will determine the treatment of emotional and behavioural problems'. There are a number of causal factors that assist in explaining unwanted behaviour, disaffection and disengagement among some pupils; these are often multivariate and overlapping. The attribution of a cause can frequently result in the

Task 3.3.2 What is unacceptable behaviour?

It is important that you arrive at a personal definition of what comprises unacceptable behaviour. Divide a blank sheet of paper into three. Head the left-hand section 'Totally unacceptable' and the right-hand section 'Acceptable'. The middle section is reserved for 'Acceptable in certain circumstances'. Now examine your own classroom teaching, and complete each section. Remember, behaviour is as much about positive learning behaviour as it is those pupil actions that you regard as unacceptable or challenging. Reflect on your responses and discuss with your tutor and record in your PDP. Should the opportunity arise, you might wish to undertake this exercise with your pupils, in order to gather their thoughts. Comparing your list to theirs is likely to prove very revealing! You may also wish to discuss your responses with another student teacher.

acquisition of a negative label by the pupil. But, on the other hand, understanding and recognising the causes can give you clues as to what might be successful strategies. A brief outline of causal factors is given below. There is more exhaustive coverage in a variety of other sources (for example, Garner *et al.* 2014).

Factors that may cause unacceptable behaviour

You should recognise that for some pupils, their unacceptable behaviour is caused by several of the factors identified below:

Individual factors

- A pupil believes that the work is not within their grasp and as a result feels embarrassed and alienated and lacks self-esteem as a learner.
- A pupil may well experience learning difficulties.
- A pupil may have mental health, stress and possible drug misuse issues, all of which are important factors explaining underachievement and inappropriate behaviour in adolescence.

Cultural factors

- Adolescence can be a period of rebellion or resistance for many young people.
- Possible tension between societal expectation and the beliefs and opinions of the pupil.
- Group/peer pressure can result in various forms of alienation to school.
- Negative experience of schooling by parents, siblings or other family members.

Curriculum relevance factors (linked to both individual and cultural)

- The curriculum may be seen by a pupil to be inaccessible and irrelevant.
- The school may give academic excellence more value than vocational qualifications or curriculum options.

School ethos and relationships factors

- ▪ Some schools can be 'deviance provocative' – their organisational structures and procedures are viewed by pupils as oppressive and negative.
- ▪ Some schools are less inclusive, both academically and socially, to pupils who behave 'differently'.

External barriers to participation and learning factors

- ▪ Family breakdown or illness usually impacts negatively on a pupil's mental health, and often on their sense of priority.
- ▪ Poverty and hardship can mean that a pupil's physiological needs are not met – such pupils may be tired, hungry and consequently easily distracted (see also Maslow 1970 in Unit 3.2).
- ▪ Sibling and caring responsibilities may mean that some pupils arrive late in your lesson – or not at all.

One aspect of causality that needs further consideration is that causal influences have been conceptualised as constituting three interlinked relationships first identified in what Bronfenbrenner (1979) called the *ecosystemic theory of relationships*. In the case of a pupil who is consistently behaving inappropriately, it is suggested that there has been a breakdown in one (or more) of these three relationships:

- ▪ pupils' relationship with themselves (how pupils feel about themselves, their self-confidence as learners and their self-esteem);
- ▪ pupils' relationship with others (how they interact socially and academically with all others in their class and school);
- ▪ pupils' relationship with the learning they are undertaking (the curriculum) (how accessible they feel a lesson is and how best they think they learn).

The interrelationship between these is shown in Figure 3.3.2.

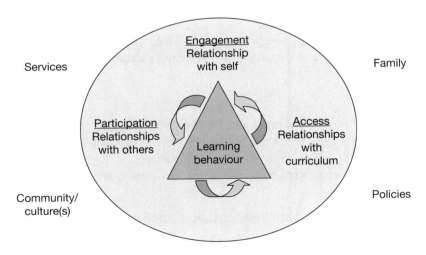

Figure 3.3.2 The behaviour for learning model

Source: After Tod and Powell (2004)

Subsequently, this theory was applied to pupil behaviour, in what was termed 'behaviour for learning' (Ellis and Tod 2009). This approach argues that all three 'relationships' need to be taken into account when planning your strategy to tackle unacceptable behaviour. The emphasis upon positive relationships is an integral component of the approach, with individual pupils as well as whole classes. This effort needs to begin from your first encounter with a group of pupils; over time, it will enable you to establish a classroom climate in which pupil learning can flourish.

Task 3.3.3 links causes to possible teaching strategies.

 Task 3.3.3 Linking causes to possible teaching strategies

Consider one pupil you are teaching who sometimes exhibits behaviour(s) unacceptable to you. Write a brief description of each of the behaviours, making sure that your language is clear and describes clearly observable pupil actions. Taking each behaviour in turn and referring to the causal factors identified above, assess which factors you feel might underlie that particular behaviour. Consider how amenable to change each of the causal factors you have identified is. Also identify any other teachers (for example, the SENCO) who might be able to provide you with advice and support. Finally, reflect on how your interpretation of cause might inform the way in which you choose to address the behaviour(s) shown.

Make notes in your PDP and discuss your responses with your tutor.

Key principles of a behaviour for learning approach

During the last six to seven years, there has been an increasing interest in the 'social and emotional aspect of learning' (SEAL). This recognises that an awareness of aspects of 'emotional intelligence' (Goleman 1995) can assist teachers in helping to create a positive climate for learning, in which good relationships between them and their pupils are paramount. It is based, in part, on the premise that 'generally a punitive approach tends to worsen or sometimes even create the very problems it is intended to eradicate ... punishment alienates children from their teachers and does nothing to build up trust that is the bedrock of relationships' (Weare 2004: 63). Crucially, and linking SEAL to the notion of 'behaviour for learning', an understanding of 'self' is a cornerstone of learner motivation. As a result, pupils can:

- ■ be effective and successful learners;
- ■ make and sustain friendships;
- ■ deal with and resolve conflict effectively and fairly;
- ■ solve problems with others or by themselves;
- ■ manage strong feelings such as frustration, anger and anxiety;
- ■ recover from setbacks and persist in the face of difficulties;
- ■ work and play cooperatively;
- ■ compete fairly and win and lose with dignity and respect for competitors.

Although each of these represents a complex undertaking, your use of them as guidelines in developing your thinking about pupil behaviour will pay rich dividends as you progress in your

A behaviour for learning approach accepts that most social and emotional aspects of learning (SEAL) are learned, and therefore can be taught or modelled by the teacher. Evidence strongly suggests that the most successful strategies for developing a positive learning environment are those that incorporate the promotion of positive relationships (Burnett 2002). As has been suggested, each of the three (interlinked) relationships is important in developing a positive learning environment in the classroom, and as a teacher you are at the very heart of orchestrating them. Although some pupils have relatively advanced 'social and emotional' skills when they arrive at school, others (often pupils who can sometimes behave unacceptably) might need support and the direct teaching of the specific skills they have not yet learned. So your task is to focus on helping to develop appropriate skills that enable each pupil to learn within a variety of learning contexts. This can be in whole-class or small-group situations in the classroom and elsewhere in the school. Some basic principles inform the way in which this can be done. These are as follows:

- Behaviour for learning is a positive description. It tells pupils what you want them to do and why this helps them to learn, rather than focusing on behaviours that you do not want in your classroom.
- It requires that you place value on (and praise appropriately) pupil behaviour that enables and maximises learning.
- Effective behaviour for learning strategies can range from high-level listening and collaborative learning skills to remaining seated for two minutes. The emphasis is upon setting targets that are reachable by pupils.

Getting the simple things right!

So far in this unit, the focus has been placed upon the underlying principles of creating a positive learning environment. But your understanding of these must coincide with a parallel focus on the strategies that you can implement practically in order to establish yourself as a teacher who can manage pupil behaviour effectively.

In the words of the government's own Expert Adviser on Behaviour, 'managing a school or a class is a complex operation and because of this complexity it is easy to fail to get the simple, but essential, things right' (DfE 2011d). To assist you in avoiding some of the more obvious pitfalls, a helpful checklist has been devised (see Figure 3.3.3).

Each of the items in the checklist will most likely become 'second nature' to you; they are commonly understood by successful teachers as being crucial to organising effective learning in their classrooms. What you will notice is that each of the recommendations in the behaviour checklist (DfE 2011d) connects well with both Bronfenbrenner's ecosystem theory and the relationships that underpin a 'behaviour for learning' approach. Now complete Task 3.3.4.

Incorporating both a set of clear principles and some straightforward actions enables you to prevent the occurrence of unacceptable behaviour by pupils. It also assists you in giving a firm and consistent response to any instances of problem behaviour that might arise. What this also does is enable you to present yourself in a classroom leadership role. Most pupils will come to your class-room wanting to learn, although there will be times when some will either be unable or unwilling to learn on account of some of the factors described earlier in this unit. In dealing with this situation, it is important to develop certain classroom leadership skills that contribute to your being able to

Classroom

- ☐ Know the names and roles of any adults in class.
- ☐ Meet and greet pupils when they come into the classroom.
- ☐ Display rules in the class – and ensure that the pupils and staff know what they are.
- ☐ Display the tariff of sanctions in class.
- ☐ Have a system in place to follow through with all sanctions.
- ☐ Display the tariff of rewards in class.
- ☐ Have a system in place to follow through with all rewards.
- ☐ Have a visual timetable on the wall.
- ☐ Follow the school behaviour policy.

Pupils

- ☐ Know the names of pupils.
- ☐ Have a plan for pupils who are likely to misbehave.
- ☐ Ensure other adults in the class know the plan.
- ☐ Understand pupils' special needs.

Teaching

- ☐ Ensure that all resources are prepared in advance.
- ☐ Praise the behaviour you want to see more of.
- ☐ Praise pupils doing the right thing more than criticising those who are doing the wrong thing (parallel praise).
- ☐ Differentiate.
- ☐ Stay calm.
- ☐ Have clear routines for transitions and for stopping the class.
- ☐ Teach pupils the class routines.

Parents

- ☐ Give feedback to parents about their child's behaviour – let them know about the good days as well as the bad ones.

Figure 3.3.3 Behaviour checklist for teachers

Source: DfE (2011d)

 Task 3.3.4 Relationships and pupil behaviour

We have noted that promoting positive behaviour requires the teacher to understand three sets of relationships, with *self*, *others* and with the *curriculum*. But we have also noted that you need to take some practical steps in order to make these relationships happen. Examine the behaviour checklist (see Figure 3.3.3) and allocate each of the items in it to one or more of these relationship areas. Reflect on their distribution, compare and discuss your findings with another student teacher and store your findings in your PDP.

establish a well-organised environment for learning, forge positive relationships with all pupils, and establish a classroom ethos that allows pupils to demonstrate positive behaviour and optimum attainment.

A classroom leader needs to address three broad elements that help to define the ethos of the classroom. While these issues are important for all pupils, they are essential elements for promoting the engagement and positive behaviour of pupils who are at risk of misbehaviour. They are:

■ Motivation: you need to provide time at the start of each lesson to tell pupils what they are learning and why. Pupils need to be involved at every stage in assessing whether these learning intentions have been met (Unit 3.2 looks at motivation in more depth).

■ Emotional well-being: to help reduce pupil anxiety, you should share the lesson structure with pupils at the start, so they know what is going to happen during the lesson.

■ Expectations: you need to give time at the start of the lesson and before each new activity to make clear what behaviours are needed for this piece of learning to be successful.

These three underpinning elements are embedded in more specific teacher actions that allow you to demonstrate your role as the classroom leader to your pupils. These include:

■ good communication between yourself and your pupils (see Unit 3.1);
■ secure subject knowledge;
■ providing lively, well-paced lessons;
■ understanding and meeting the learning needs of all pupils in your class;
■ acting on your reflections and evaluations of previous lessons (feedback loop) (see also Unit 2.1);
■ demonstrating confidence and direction in managing pupils;
■ modelling desired behaviours yourself.

It is unlikely that, as a student teacher, everything clicks into place straight away; some of these will develop with experience. Nevertheless, it is worth noting that research has shown that student teachers who display confidence in managing their classes are less likely to encounter problem behaviour by pupils (Giallo and Little 2003).

Building positive relationships in classrooms

As has been discussed earlier in this unit, promoting positive behaviour places emphasis on the relationships you form with your pupils. Ineffective interventions are usually the product of unsatisfactory relationships with individual pupils. These interventions, even though they are ultimately unsuccessful, take up valuable teaching time and impact negatively on the learning of an individual pupil, the rest of the class, and also on your own confidence. Most interventions should take the form of positive actions that fit somewhere on a continuum from *positive reinforcement* through to *positive correction*. The actions you select should be those that enable learning to continue. They usually include eye contact, use of pupil name, description of the appropriate behaviour you would like the pupil to demonstrate, praise and affirmation (see also Units 3.1 and 3.2). For example:

- modelling appropriate behaviour;
- positive reinforcement and the appropriate use of targeted praise;
- consistent and firm application of rules;
- use of verbal and non-verbal communication;
- listening to pupils and respecting their opinions;
- remaining vigilant (pre-empting unacceptable behaviour);
- dealing decisively with lateness and non-attendance.

By consistently using these approaches in your teaching, you are more likely to forge meaningful and positive relationships with your pupils. In sum, effective relationships mean that there is common ground between pupil and teacher. This is as vital in securing appropriate conditions for learning as it is for managing those behavioural issues that may be potentially problematic.

Structuring your lessons to promote positive behaviour

The design of effective lessons is fundamental to high-quality teaching and learning, and is vital to the job of promoting positive behaviour; the government's behaviour checklist provides a baseline set of headings that you need to take into account in doing this. As the commentary on the checklist states:

> Teachers who follow these guidelines find there is more consistency of approach to managing behaviour, both in the classroom and around the school. When children know that teachers will stick to the behaviour policy and class routines, they feel safer and happy, and behaviour improves.

> (DfE 2011d: 1)

As a result, pupil behaviour, as well as their learning, will improve. Effective lesson design takes into account behavioural differences between pupils as much as it does their levels of achievement or the subject or skill they are learning. Your teaching should be characterised by:

- focus and structure so that pupils are clear about what is to be learned and how it fits with what they know already;
- actively engaging pupils in their learning so that they make their own meaning from it;
- developing pupils' learning skills systematically so that their learning becomes increasingly independent (see also Unit 5.2);
- using assessment for learning to help pupils reflect on what they already know, reinforce the learning being developed and set targets for the future (Units 6.1 and 6.2 discuss assessment);
- having high expectations of the effort that pupils should make and what they can achieve (see also Unit 3.2);
- motivating pupils by well-paced lessons, using stimulating activities matched to a range of learning styles that encourage attendance;
- creating an environment that promotes learning in a settled and purposeful atmosphere.

You can further promote a positive approach to behaviour by building individual teaching sequences within an overall lesson. The lesson (or a sequence of lessons) needs first of all to be firmly located, in the mind of the pupil, in the context of: (a) a scheme of work; (b) pupils' prior knowledge; and (c) their preferred learning styles. It is also important to identify clear learning outcomes. Structuring your lesson as a series of 'episodes' by separating pupil learning into distinct stages or steps, and then planning how each step should be taught, enables those pupils who are at risk of distraction or lack of concentration to regard the lesson as a series of 'bite-sized chunks'. Finally, you can secure overall coherence by providing: (a) a stimulating start to the lesson; (b) transition 'signposts' between each lesson episode, which reviews pupil learning so far and launches the next episode; and (c) a final plenary session that reviews learning (lesson planning is covered in Unit 2.2).

Rights, responsibilities, routines and rules

A framework for promoting positive classroom behaviour has been commonly constructed around the so-called 4Rs: rights, responsibilities, rules and routines (Hook and Vass 2000). You should recognise that such a focus operates best within the context of a fifth 'R', already encountered in this unit – 'relationships'. In applying aspects of the 4Rs, you need to be very sensitive, as a student teacher, to the existing arrangements in any class that you work in – these will have been established over a long period of time by the permanent class teacher. But you can begin by being conscious of how each of these 'Rs' can have a positive impact on your teaching.

Rights (R1) and responsibilities (R2)

Both rights and responsibilities are inextricably linked. They refer equally to teacher and pupils, and are the basis on which classroom relationships, teaching and learning are built.

■ Teacher's responsibilities – you must seek to enable all pupils to learn, to seek out and celebrate improvements in learning, to treat pupils with respect and to create a positive classroom environment in which pupils feel safe and able to learn.
■ Teacher's rights – you must be allowed to teach with a minimum of hindrance, to feel safe, to be supported by colleagues and to be listened to.
■ Pupils' responsibilities – pupils must be willing to learn, to allow others to learn, to cooperate with teaching and other staff and peers, and to do their best at all times.
■ Pupils' rights – pupils should be treated with respect, be safe, be able to learn and be listened to.

Rules (R3)

These are the mechanisms by which rights and responsibilities are translated into adult and pupil behaviours. They are best constructed collaboratively, so that the views of all pupils are taken into account.

Routines (R4)

These are the structures that underpin the rules and reinforce the smooth running of the classroom. The more habitual the routines become, the more likely they are to be used. Pupils who behave inappropriately often do so because they are unsure of what is happening in the classroom at a given time. Consistent application of your classroom rules will constitute a major step in establishing a routine in your class.

In using the 4Rs as a basis for promoting positive pupils, you should be encouraged to provide opportunities for your pupils to make choices about their behaviour, thus allowing them to take responsibility for their own actions. Choice is guided by their responsibilities and leads to positive or negative consequences according to the choice made by the pupil.

Consequences

Pupils need to know the consequences of sensible or inadvisable choices. Responsible choices lead to positive consequences; conversely, a choice to behave inappropriately leads to a known negative consequence.

Now complete Task 3.3.5, which is designed to help you to focus on the ways you use encouragement, positive feedback and praise in the classroom, and Task 3.3.6, which focuses on the impact of praise on your pupils.

In Task 3.3.7, you are asked to explore the links between behaviour and learning. Task 3.3.8 asks you to consider different definitions of unacceptable behaviour.

 Task 3.3.5 Monitoring your use of praise and encouragement in the classroom

A very useful starting point to promote the notion of positive approaches to behaviour is to examine the ways in which you provide encouragement, positive feedback and praise to your pupils. You can assess this by developing a log of praise and encouragement to use as a tool for measuring these positive interactions.

Add to the list of positive pupil behaviours identified below, which you can use to give praise. Underneath each one, note the words or actions you might use to convey to the pupil that your recognition carries value and meaning in that they are clearly directed towards a particular pupil and are linked to the positive behaviour that the pupil has demonstrated.

1   Queuing sensibly and quietly to enter the classroom.
2   Allowing another pupil to go first.
3   Lending an item of equipment to another pupil.
4   Putting waste paper in the bin.
5   Supporting another pupil's learning.
6   _____
7   _____
8   _____
9   _____
10 _____

During your observation of a lesson taught by a more experienced teacher in your placement school, record other ways in which that teacher acknowledges positive behaviour by pupils. Compare your notes on this topic with another student teacher working in a different setting. Store in your PDP for later reference.

Task 3.3.6 The impact of praise

Undertake a small-scale project designed to establish the impact of 'praise' on pupils in your class. In doing this, you should: (a) develop one or more research questions, so that your data collection has a focus; (b) identify a small, but recent and relevant, set of literature that contributes to a theoretical understanding of the issue; (c) define and provide a rationale for your methodology (including coverage of any ethical issues that might emerge in such a study); (d) gather and analyse data; and (e) consider the relevance of your findings to your practice. Store this in your PDP.

Among the possible research questions you might wish to consider are:

- Do boys prefer different kinds of praise and encouragement than girls?
- Does the nature and type of praise change according to age?
- What types of praise do pupils prefer?
- Is praise evenly distributed among your teaching group?
- Is praise carefully targeted and in response to specific pupil actions?
- Does personal praise link closely with a whole-school approach?

 Task 3.3.7 Exploring further the links between behaviour and learning

To explore further the links between behaviour and learning, select one or more pupils who you currently teach in your placement school and who present you with a particular challenge on account of their unacceptable behaviour. You should explore the learning and behaviour interface by responding to the following key questions:

- Does the educational achievement of this pupil vary from one curriculum subject to another?
- What are the characteristics of those curriculum subjects in which the pupil appears to perform more effectively?
- Has the pattern of educational achievement been inconsistent over time? Are there any logical explanations for this?
- Do you know anything about the pupil's preferred learning style?
- What are your own views about the capabilities of this pupil?
- What do other subject teachers say about the educational achievements of this pupil?

Each of the above questions can form the basis of a small-scale classroom enquiry. For each, you could: (a) gather evidence from the school's pupil data; (b) obtain information from key personnel (for instance, the pupil's form tutor, or the SENCO); and (c) secure inputs from the pupil directly (subject to the appropriate permissions).

On the basis of what you discover, try to formulate a theoretical model for both the unacceptable behaviours displayed and their relationship with more positive aspects of this pupil's school performance. Store this in your PDP.

Task 3.3.8 Interpretations of unacceptable behaviour

Interpretations of 'unacceptable behaviour', and the ways in which it has been defined, have changed over time. In spite of this, the educational literature is replete with material (research papers, books, official reports and guidance documents) looking at ways in which schools and teachers can manage behaviour more effectively. Two examples of this, separated by nearly 20 years, are the Elton Report (1989) and the Steer Report (2005). Using the links provided below, consider the similarities and differences in the recommendations of each report. What does the content of these documents tell you about official policy on pupil behaviour? Are there many commonalities regarding the practical advice that these reports offer to classroom teachers? Are you able to draw any inferences from the generic commentaries given concerning the nature and extent of pupil behaviour in schools?

Write up your analysis, discuss with your tutor or other student teachers and store in your PDP.

The Elton Report is available at: http://www.educationengland.org.uk/documents/elton/elton1989.html

The Steer Report is available at: www.educationengland.org.uk/documents/pdfs/2005-steer-report-learning-behaviour.pdf

SUMMARY AND KEY POINTS

■ Adopting a positive approach to managing pupil behaviour is crucially important.

■ Become familiar with your school's policies regarding behaviour management.

■ Take steps to understand what are the underlying causes of the problem behaviour in your class – this is the first step in taking positive action.

■ Try to establish a clear set of classroom rules and rewards and sanctions, and ensure that they are applied consistently and fairly.

■ Focus on your relationships with pupils – establishing an effective working relationship is crucial to a positive classroom 'ethos'.

■ Always try to lead by example – try to model the kinds of positive behaviours you want to see from your pupils.

■ Seek guidance and support from more experienced teachers in your school, and make use of all opportunities for professional development.

Check which requirements for your ITE programme you have addressed through this unit.

Further reading

Ellis, S. and Tod, J. (2014) *Promoting Behaviour for Learning in the Classroom*, London: Routledge.
This book provides a concise analysis of established behaviour management strategies that you can use in your own classroom. It recognises that no single approach will work for *all* pupils and that it is important to understand the individual needs, attributes and personalities of your pupils when deciding how best to intervene. The book covers a range of issues, including developing positive relationships in the classroom, understanding personal style and self-management, making use of effective feedback and rewards, individual differences and special educational needs, and dealing with challenging behaviour.

Haydn, T. (2012) *Managing Pupil Behaviour: Improving the Classroom Atmosphere*, 2nd edn, London: Routledge.
This book provides some very practical insights into how best you can manage behaviour effectively in your classroom. It will encourage you to think about the degree to which you are relaxed and in assured control of your class – so that you can really enjoy your teaching.
Managing Pupil Behaviour uses the views of over 140 teachers and 700 pupils to provide insights into the factors that enable teachers to manage learning effectively in their classrooms. It argues that this enables pupils to learn and achieve. Key issues explored include the factors that influence the working atmosphere in the classroom, the impact of that atmosphere on teaching and learning, and tensions around inclusive practice and situations where some pupils may be spoiling the learning of others.

Rogers, W. (2011) *Classroom Behaviour: A Practical Guide to Effective Teaching, Behaviour Management and Colleague Support*, London: Sage.
This book explores some of the issues that you will face when working in today's classrooms. It describes real situations and dilemmas and offers advice on dealing with the challenges of the job. Emphasis is placed on how to establish and enhance your relationships with pupils. The book also considers some more specialist aspects of teaching pupils who have additional needs, including sections looking at dealing with bullying, teaching students on the autistic spectrum in a mainstream classroom and working with very challenging students.

Roffey, S. (2010) *Changing Behaviour in Schools*, London: Sage.
This book will show you how to promote positive behaviour and well-being in your classroom. It provides examples of effective strategies for encouraging prosocial and collaborative behaviour in the classroom, the school and the wider community. It emphasises the importance of the social and emotional aspects of learning and introduces the idea that pupils should develop a sense of belonging in the classroom. Each chapter has case studies from primary and secondary schools, activities, checklists and suggestions for further reading.

Other resources and websites

Key policy documents relating to pupil behaviour

Improving behaviour and attendance in schools
www.gov.uk/government/policies/improving-behaviour-and-attendance-in-schools
Status: Departmental Policy, August 2014

Behaviour and discipline in schools: advice to headteachers and school staff
www.gov.uk/government/publications/behaviour-and-discipline-in-schools
Status: Departmental advice, September 2014

Getting the simple things right: Charlie Taylor's behaviour checklists: www.education.gov.uk/schools/
pupilsupport/behaviour/a00199342/getting-the-simple-thingsright-charlie-taylors-behaviour-checklists
Status: Departmental advice, April 2012

Guidance for governing bodies on behaviour and discipline
www.gov.uk/government/publications/behaviour-and-discipline-in-schools-guidance-for-governing-bodies
Status: Statutory guidance, July 2013

Use of reasonable force
www.gov.uk/government/publications/use-of-reasonable-force-in-schools
Status: Departmental advice, July 2013

Screening, searching and confiscation
www.gov.uk/government/publications/searching-screening-and-confiscation
Status: Departmental advice (February 2014)

Preventing and tackling bullying
www.gov.uk/government/publications/preventing-and-tackling-bullying
Status: Departmental advice, November 2014

Appendix 2 on pages 591–595 provides further examples of websites you may find useful.

Capel, S., Leask, M. and Turner, T. (eds) (2010) *Readings for Learning to Teach in the Secondary School: A Companion to M Level Study*, London: Routledge.
This book brings together essential readings to support you in your critical engagement with key issues raised in this textbook.

The subject-specific books in the Routledge *Learning to Teach* series are also very useful.

Any additional resources and an editable version of any relevant tasks/tables in this unit are available on the companion website: www.routledge.com/cw/capel

---

Chapter 6

Effective use of positive feedback and rewards

Introduction

The need for teachers to focus on positive behaviour is well established in national guidance on behaviour. The Elton Report made the point that evidence gathered from literature and through the enquiry itself suggested that teachers should 'emphasise the positive, including praise for good behaviour as well as good work' (DES 1989: 72), and make sparing and consistent use of reprimands and sanctions. The point that praise should be available for behaviour as well as academic learning was reinforced by the Steer Report's (DfES 2005a) observation that, while many schools had excellent systems to reward good work and behaviour, there were some that relied on sanctions to enforce good behaviour but neglected the use of appropriate rewards.

Reflecting the consistent message of the need to recognise and reinforce positive behaviour, guidance on school discipline and pupil behaviour policies issued by the Labour Government stated: 'It has long been established that rewards are more effective than punishment in motivating pupils. By praising and rewarding positive behaviour, others will be encouraged to act similarly' (DCSF 2009a: 27).

The document also suggested that a rewards/sanctions ratio of at least 5:1 was an indication of a school with an effective rewards and sanctions system. The origins of this suggestion are not entirely clear, although the DCSF document attributes it to the Elton Report. Whatever the origins, the ratio reinforces the message that there is a need to place emphasis on recognising and acknowledging positive behaviour through the use of praise and other forms of reward.

The current Teachers' Standards (DfE 2011a: 8–9) require teachers to 'establish a framework for discipline with a range of strategies, using praise, sanctions and rewards consistently and fairly'. This chapter encourages you to think beyond the simple and generally accepted need to 'be more positive' and consider how praise and rewards can be provided effectively in line with the principles of the behaviour for learning approach.

Positive feedback and reward in the context of the behaviour for learning approach

From a behaviour for learning perspective, the purpose of praise and rewards (and the positive correction and sanctions discussed in the next chapter) is to foster the development of positive learning behaviours. For many pupils the standard diet of rewards and sanctions, together with an eclectic mix of other routine practices, achieves this (or at least does not hinder it). Inevitably for some, it does not. The B4L approach explicitly recognises this and, through the core and extended use described in Chapter 1, provides a means of responding, either by a more explicit focus on the desirable learning behaviours or by targeting one or more of the behaviour for learning relationships.

Within the B4L approach, praise is conceptualised as the provision of verbal encouragement that is focused on the learning behaviours exhibited. It can be thought of as the provision for the pupil of feedback on their behavioural performance. For this reason and some others we explore in the next section, our preference is for the term 'positive feedback' rather than 'praise'. When a reward is given, we would always expect positive feedback to accompany it so that the pupil still receives information on their performance. Positive feedback can contribute to the pupil's relationship with self by letting them know that their positive learning behaviours have been noticed and are valued. It is important for a teacher to recognise and respond differently to the exceptions, but most pupils, like adults, will like to hear when they have done something well.

When a teacher feeds back positively, it also has a potential impact on the pupil's relationship with others. Even in an interaction with a pupil over their compliance with a basic expectation, the positive feedback does not just relate to the behaviour: it conveys a message about the teacher–pupil relationship. For example, when a teacher acknowledges that a pupil has remembered their planner, they are also implicitly affirming to them 'I do notice when you get things right'. Such an interaction lets the pupil know that they are in a relationship with a teacher who recognises and values their efforts, rather than a relationship that is based on fault finding and criticism.

However, although many pupils may experience positive feedback in this way, a note of caution should also be sounded here. The pupil's relationship with others does not just include their relationship with their teacher. Adopting a B4L approach involves selecting and evaluating strategies rather than expecting to follow a recipe for best practice. For some pupils, their relationship with peers may be damaged by receiving positive feedback or a reward from the teacher because to be seen to gain teacher approval is not desirable. Consideration therefore needs to be given to the way in which feedback is given. For example, it may need to be given more privately or in a depersonalised way.

Finally, the positive feedback can also provide reinforcement of the learning behaviours associated with the pupil's relationship with the curriculum. For example, the teacher might positively recognise the pupil's personal organisation or their problem-solving strategies when they encountered a difficult part of the task.

Positive feedback rather than praise

Although 'praise' is the term that is in common usage (e.g. DfE 2011a, 2014a; TA 2012) our preference is for the phrase 'positive feedback'. We would argue that, when the term 'praise' is applied in an educational context, it needs to be understood as referring to positive feedback. If praise is interpreted in the more conventional, publicly accepted sense, there is an implication that the act that attracts it is of a significant magnitude to be deserving of a high level of approval, admiration or commendation. We might, for example, hear on the news of a member of the public praised for their quick thinking and bravery in an emergency situation. This person is very different from a pupil who has, for example, remembered to put their hand up rather than calling out, or has remembered to bring the right equipment to a lesson. We believe that this is why some teachers find it difficult to accept the idea of praising pupils; it seems incongruous to *praise* a pupil for conforming to basic expectations, especially those that many others routinely follow. However, giving *feedback* on performance is something teachers do regularly and necessarily in relation to learning. We would suggest that we need to think in terms of *feedback* in relation to behaviour as well. With older pupils in particular, using a phrase like 'Fantastic, John, you've remembered to put your hand up' may seem insincere to the praise giver, the praise receiver and the observers. However, in the same situation we could say, 'John, thanks for waiting, how can I help?' This provides positive feedback on performance and conveys, in a low-key way, that the teacher notices when a pupil demonstrates the required behaviour.

What do we know about effective positive feedback?

O'Leary and O'Leary (1977, cited in Brophy 1981: 12) indicated that teacher praise must have the following qualities to function effectively as reinforcement:

1   Contingency: the praise must be contingent on performance of the behaviour to be reinforced.
2   Specificity: the praise should specify the particulars of the behaviour being reinforced.
3   Sincerity/variety/credibility: the praise should sound sincere. Among other things, this means that the content will be varied according to the situation and the preferences of the student being praised.

In a seminal piece of work on the use of praise by teachers, Brophy (1981: 12) drew on a range of studies, including O'Leary and O'Leary's (1977) work, to make the distinctions between effective and ineffective praise shown in Table 6.1.

Brophy (1981) was referring to all uses of praise, not just in relation to behaviour. Informed by Brophy's suggestions, we would stress the following key points when using positive feedback to promote the development of learning behaviour:

- Feedback to individuals is provided within the context of a whole class approach where desirable learning behaviours are known, explicitly referred to and regularly reinforced.
- Phrase the feedback so that it is descriptive, providing information to the pupil on the learning behaviour they have exhibited that has drawn this positive attention. In the case of public positive feedback, this also allows other members of the class to hear information about the desirable learning behaviours.
- The feedback can be purely descriptive (e.g. 'John, I can see you are sitting up ready to listen') but if there is an evaluative element (e.g. 'Well done') it should form only a small proportion of the message.
- If a teacher just uses the evaluative element (e.g. 'Good', 'Fantastic', 'Well done') without a descriptive component, they are missing an opportunity to convey information to the pupil concerned and, if publicly given, others too about the desired learning behaviours.
- Positive feedback needs to be available for effort, improvement and achievements in both learning and behaviour.
- Within the positive feedback, any reference to the reasons for success should relate to factors the pupil can influence (e.g. their effort, sustained attention to the task) on future occasions.

120

Table 6.1 Effective and ineffective praise (Brophy 1981: 26)

Effective Praise		Ineffective Praise	
1	Is delivered contingently	1	Is delivered randomly or unsystematically
2	Specifies the particulars of the accomplishment	2	Is restricted to global positive reactions
3	Shows spontaneity, variety and other signs of credibility; suggests clear attention to the student's accomplishment	3	Shows a bland uniformity, which suggests a conditioned response made with minimal attention
4	Rewards attainment of specified performance criteria (which can include effort criteria, however)	4	Rewards mere participation, without consideration of performance processes or outcomes
5	Provides information to students about their competence or the value of their accomplishments	5	Provides no information at all or gives students little information about their status
6	Orients students towards better appreciation of their own task-related behaviour and thinking about problem solving	6	Orients students towards comparing themselves with others and thinking about competing
7	Uses students' own prior accomplishments as the context for describing present accomplishments	7	Uses the accomplishment of peers as the context for describing students' present accomplishments
8	Is given in recognition of noteworthy effort or success (for *this* student) in relation to tasks	8	Is given without regard to the effort expended or the meaning of the accomplishment (for *this* student)
9	Attributes success to effort and ability, implying that similar successes can be expected in the future	9	Attributes success to ability alone or to external factors such as luck or easy task
10	Fosters endogenous attributions (students believe that they expend effort on the task because they enjoy the task and/or want to develop task-relevant skills)	10	Fosters exogenous attributions (students believe that they expend effort on the task for external reasons – to please the teacher, win a competition or reward, etc.)
11	Focuses students' attention on their own task-relevant behaviour	11	Focuses students' attention on the teacher as an external authority figure who is manipulating them
12	Fosters appreciation of and desirable attributions about task-relevant behaviour after the process is completed	12	Intrudes into the ongoing process, distracting attention from task-relevant behaviour

- Positive feedback should not be used in a way that is likely to be experienced as manipulative, insincere or 'all technique and no substance'.
- Positive feedback should not be 'overblown' – remembering basic equipment is worthy of positive acknowledgement (e.g. 'Good to see you've remembered your . . . ') but more than this may be experienced as patronising or insincere.
- Don't mix positive feedback with negative feedback. Human nature is to dwell on the negative component even if this only represents a small proportion of the overall

message. For example, if your aim is to reinforce settling to the starter activity, you would avoid a statement like 'You got on really quickly with the starter, it's such a shame that you . . . '

- Avoid the 'giveth and taketh away' approach of saying, for example, 'You've worked really hard today . . . for a change' or 'I see you've remembered your planner . . . at last'.

Remembering to give positive feedback

The Elton Report (DES 1989) contained the comment that 'in some schools a pupil can only get attention in one or other of two ways – by working well or behaving badly' (DES 1989: 99). Although 25 years old, this is still an observation that it is important to consider as a teacher in terms of monitoring and evaluating both the overall classroom climate you are creating and the experience of individuals within your class.

We have already covered one reason why some teachers may find it difficult to be more positive in the classroom. It may be that praising a behaviour that could reasonably be considered a basic expectation seems unnecessary. It is hoped that focusing on the notion of positive feedback will help in reconciling such concerns by drawing a parallel with the approach we would use to encourage learning. Canter and Canter (1992), the originators of the Assertive Discipline approach, put forward another argument as to why it may be difficult for teachers to remember to focus on and acknowledge positive behaviour. They had found through their observations that 90% of teachers' comments to pupils regarding behaviour were negative. Canter and Canter (1992) explained this by using an anxiety scale. They suggested that at 0 the teacher's anxiety is so low that they are probably asleep, 100 on the scale represents a panic attack and 50 the normal anxiety level within the classroom. If a pupil loudly disrupts or refuses to do as they are asked, then the teacher's anxiety level rises. Canter and Canter (1992) argued that there is a physiological reaction to a perceived threat that prompts the teacher to act to lower the anxiety that is currently causing a degree of discomfort. The action might be a verbal reprimand or the threat or imposition of a sanction. The physiological response when pupils are behaving well may be a drop in the teacher's anxiety level. As Canter and Canter (1992: 61) put it, 'There is no voice in your head telling you to do something immediately. No panic. No sense of urgency.' The suggestion in some texts (e.g. DfES 2005a; Dix 2007) that there should be a ratio of at least five positive comments to every negative comment is helpful as a reminder that may compensate for what Canter and Canter (1992) suggested is a natural tendency to react strongly to misbehaviour but give insufficient attention to positive behaviour.

Although ratios provide a quantitative means of monitoring teacher positivity within the classroom and reinforce the important message that teachers should focus more attention on the positive, it should be recognised that not all positive feedback necessarily carries equal weight. Positive feedback from someone who is important to the pupil and whose opinion they respect is likely to be more significant. The quality of the existing teacher–pupil relationship is therefore an important variable. A single piece of positive feedback from someone with whom you have a good relationship and whose opinion you respect may carry more weight than several pieces of positive feedback from someone for whom you have little regard.

Activity 6.1

This activity is intended to give a broad indication of your positivity within the classroom. Because you know this, you may be more positive than you would normally be. This is a known effect and does not matter – as with pupils who seem to behave well when they are being observed, it at least shows the behaviour is in your repertoire!

- Draw a seating plan of your class, ensuring that under each pupil's name there is space for recording. Have an additional box somewhere on the paper headed 'Comments to the class or groups'.
- Ask a colleague with whom you have a good relationship to observe one of your lessons.
- On the classroom plan, your colleague should use a simple code to record under a pupil's name any comments you directed to them. The code should cover:
    - o positive behaviour-related comments
    - o negative behaviour-related comments
    - o positive learning-related comments
    - o negative learning-related comments.

The same four categories should be used for 'Comments to the class or groups'.

- Before the observation you should agree on how certain interactions will be recorded. For example, some learning-related comments will simply be instructional. You may agree that these will be excluded, you might have an additional neutral category or you could decide that any comment that is not negative should be recorded as positive. In the next chapter, we talk about positive correction. For example, you might say, 'John, facing this way, thanks' as an alternative to 'John, stop turning round'. Although the wording is positive, this is still responding to unwanted behaviour, so you might decide this sort of comment is still classed as 'negative behaviour related'. Remember, however, that this is not a statistical exercise, nor is it intended that you should compare yourself with anyone else, so absolute consistency in recording is not required. It is just helpful to the observer to have some idea in advance of how to record these examples when there might be an element of doubt.
- Look at the results of the observation. Consider questions such as:
    - o What is the balance between the different categories of comment overall?
    - o How many positive behaviour-related comments did you make compared with negative behaviour-related comments?
    - o Are there some individuals who received no comments of any kind from you?
    - o Are there some pupils who received only negative behaviour-related comments from you?

(continued)

(continued)

> o Does the plan reveal sections of the room where most of the comments were negative behaviour-related comments?
>
> o Are there gender differences reflected in the distribution of the different types of comment?
>
> • Of course, one reaction when you see that a pupil has received a number of negative behaviour-related comments might be that this was the result of the behaviour they chose to exhibit. This may be true but, if we think in terms of relationships and what it is like to be the pupil, there would be a concern if the only interactions with adults they experienced lesson after lesson and day after day were of this nature. There would be a need to consider carefully how positive aspects of the pupil's learning and behaviour, however small, could be identified and remarked upon.

Tailoring praise to individuals

As adults we may assume positive feedback to be, as its name suggests, a positive experience for pupils. The underlying principle is that, if a required behaviour is positively reinforced by something that the pupil finds rewarding, they will be more likely to exhibit that behaviour again in the future. If this is a major purpose of providing positive feedback, then it makes sense to attempt to deliver any positive comment in a form that the pupil prefers and is likely to experience positively.

Public or private positive feedback

Some pupils prefer public acknowledgement; others prefer their positive feedback to be low key and one to one. The choice of strategy for reinforcing behaviour needs to be based on a prediction of how the individual is likely to experience it. If they experience public positive feedback as embarrassing and/or a threat to their social standing within their peer group, then their interpretation may be that it is not positively reinforcing at all.

Depersonalising positive feedback

We have already touched on the possibility that some pupils may find it difficult to accept praise, and suggested that a stronger emphasis on the descriptive component within positive feedback may help. However, an alternative for those pupils who experience difficulty in accepting even the types of comments that include just a positive inference is to depersonalise the positive feedback. For example, as an alternative to singling out an individual, a teacher could say, 'This group's worked well together. I liked the way you all took turns using the equipment. That's good collaboration.' Or 'I'm pleased to see everyone on this table's settled down and got their equipment out.' The hope would be that the individual pupil would make the connection themselves that this positive comment applied to them as much as the others.

Reducing the evaluative component even further

As we have indicated, effective positive feedback involves a descriptive element that gives the pupil information on the behaviour they have exhibited that has gained this positive attention. The evaluative element of the message (e.g. 'Good', 'Well done'), if one is included at all, represents quite a small proportion of the message. Some pupils may find it particularly difficult to accept positive feedback that contains any evaluative component. For example, a pupil with low self-esteem might find it hard to accept a comment such as 'Well done, you kept your cool and put forward your argument when others in the group disagreed with you', or 'Well done, you were sharing really nicely', because such strong positive messages may not fit with how they view themselves. Coopersmith (1967) suggested that individuals, when confronted with evidence they are better or worse than they themselves have decided, generally resolve any dissonance between this evidence and their own view of themselves in favour of their customary judgement. The pupil may, for example, attempt to resolve the experienced dissonance between their customary judgement and a positive evaluative comment by attributing externally (e.g. the teacher is just saying it but doesn't really mean it) or by taking some action (e.g. destroying their work or misbehaving) that attracts peer and adult reactions more consistent with their own view of themselves. As an alternative strategy the teacher could use a solely descriptive comment such as 'You settled really quickly to the starter today'. It would be more difficult for the pupil to reject this because it is simply a statement of fact and contains less of an implication that an evaluation is being made.

Positive feedback to the whole class

Following the principle of five positives for every negative will help to maintain a more positive atmosphere within the classroom. In the next chapter we will cover positive correction as a way of ensuring that, even on those occasions when you need to address unwanted behaviour, you can do so in a way that keeps the focus on the required behaviours. There will be times, however, when it is appropriate to provide some positive feedback to the class as a whole. Similar principles apply to those when providing positive feedback to individuals. Keep the focus on a description of the behaviour and frame the evaluative comment in terms of its effect on you. For example, at the end of an activity you might say, before moving on to the next activity or further instructions, 'I'm really pleased with how well you all listened while other people were feeding back on their experiments.' Such a statement indicates the effect on the teacher ('I'm really pleased') and the learning behaviour (listening while others fed back). However, we do not want to over-complicate this process or imply that it should be treated in a formulaic way. At the close of the lesson, a secondary teacher might simply say, 'Good lesson today, everybody. Look forward to seeing you next week.'

This is not overblown praise that says the pupils were brilliant or fantastic simply for doing what was required of them; it simply acknowledges that their individual contributions made it a collectively successful, and possibly enjoyable, experience.

Making effective use of rewards

Schools vary in the extent to which the class teacher is afforded the opportunity to develop their own class-based system of rewards. In some schools, there is a whole school system to which teachers are expected to adhere. For example, in a primary school a teacher might be expected to give out merits that, once a certain number is reached, lead to a head teacher's award. It is important that you find out your own school's system and work within it.

A taxonomy of rewards

The positive feedback already discussed is a form of reward. We would also include non-verbal signals of approval such as a smile or a thumbs up. A range of rewards commonly used by schools are listed in Chapter 5. Here, however, we move on to consider some of the principles associated with the effective use of rewards. It is useful to consider first where particular forms of reward fit within an overall taxonomy of rewards:

- Intrinsic rewards: an intrinsic reward is the most educationally desirable kind of reward. By intrinsic reward, we mean the kind of pleasure and satisfaction that a pupil gets from the work they are engaged in.
- Experience of success or making progress: this is the feeling of satisfaction experienced when a task is completed successfully or steps towards the end goal are achieved.
- Other people's praise or approval: this can be verbal, such as the positive feedback we have talked about in this chapter, or non-verbal, such as a smile.
- Preferred activities: in general, the opportunity to engage in a preferred activity will serve as a reward for engaging in a less desired activity.
- Token rewards: these include things such as house points, stars and stickers. They are referred to as tokens because they have no value in themselves, but represent something else that is valued. Sometimes the value of the token is that it represents success or another person's approval. As we have previously suggested, tokens may stand alone or be part of a system where a certain number of tokens collected leads to a particular reward.
- Tangible rewards: these include things such as sweets, small toys and vouchers with financial value.

(based on McPhillimy 1996)

As is perhaps immediately evident, applying the notions of intrinsic reward and the experience of success or making progress is more difficult when thinking about pupil behaviour. Intrinsic reward needs to be interpreted as demonstrating particular behaviours based on the understanding that it is right and proper to behave in this way rather than because a reward is on offer. We could, of course, debate at length what right and proper means and for whom, but for simplicity we will make the assumption that there are some generally accepted expectations in society of how people should behave towards each other and that adhering to these requires individuals to balance their own needs with those of the wider community.

The experience of success or making progress within the taxonomy of rewards is a little easier to relate to behaviour and certainly the positive feedback we have talked about in this chapter is a helpful means of contributing to this. However, behaviour is often evaluated in terms of the reduction or cessation of certain misbehaviours. While this is a form of progress, a key principle underpinning the B4L approach is that we should draw more parallels with learning. Typically with learning we focus on and encourage through positive feedback the development of and eventual mastery of skills. We should do the same for behaviour; if we can do this, then it is possible for the pupil to recognise their progress in this area.

With regard to tangible rewards in the taxonomy, we would suggest that teachers should think carefully and consult with colleagues about whether this approach is appropriate and necessary. Having attractive pencils or rubbers on offer as a reward when a pupil reaches a certain number of points may not cause too much concern, but offering sweets, for example, could be in conflict with the school's healthy eating policy. We are aware of a number of secondary schools that use shopping vouchers, cinema tickets or theme park tickets as part of their reward system and presumably find these effective motivators. We would suggest that the use of such high-level tangible rewards is not an approach to be adopted unilaterally by an individual teacher – not least because every so often a story hits the press about the use of such approaches. Typically such stories are not positive, name the school and go along the line of questioning why pupils are being given shopping vouchers, cinema tickets or theme park tickets just for turning up and behaving themselves.

McPhillimy (1996) makes the point that the higher level of rewards, such as intrinsic rewards, are educationally preferable. This is an interesting point to consider because most school systems are characterised by forms of token reward. However, an important aspect of the taxonomy of rewards is that often different levels of reward are used simultaneously. For example, if a pupil is given the opportunity to engage in a preferred activity as a result of maintaining attention on a less favoured task for a period of time, or awarded a sticker, the teacher can supply some positive feedback that helps the pupil to recognise what they have achieved. Although intrinsic motivation may be the aim, we would suggest that some supplementary extrinsic motivation in the form of positive feedback or a reward will not diminish this for those who are already functioning at this level. As we have remarked previously, in the context of a relationship it is simply a way for the teacher to indicate that they still notice and appreciate the pupil's efforts. Similarly, if positive feedback focused on learning behaviour is used (rather than bland praise) and accompanies any rewards given, we believe this does not reduce the chance of pupils developing intrinsic motivation. By providing this type of feedback, the teacher mediates the learning from the experience of receiving the reward. For some individuals, the positive feedback and rewards may be important in maintaining a level of behaviour that allows them to start developing intrinsic motivation as they come to realise that getting their work done, not getting into trouble and the more positive relationships they are able to build bring their own benefits.

Some rewards are simply standalone indicators of approval. For example, a young child might be given a sticker. Others, such as the example given previously of a merit system that leads to a head teacher's award, are based on the idea of working towards a longer term goal. With younger children in particular, a consideration may be whether they are able to connect several events for which they have received a token with a head teacher's certificate given out later. No doubt most individuals would be pleased to receive the certificate, just as they were to achieve the merits that led to it, but whether they necessarily appreciate that the string of merits is an indication they have behaved consistently well and are therefore deserving of the head teacher's certificate may be questionable. There is a case for directly teaching pupils what the different stages of a system such as this represent. Ideally, we would like the pupil to be able to give a developmentally appropriate answer to the question 'What did you get that for?' if asked about their reward.

Taking away rewards once given

Rewards that have been given should not be taken away from groups or individuals if a subsequent piece of misbehaviour occurs. The reason is that the positive behaviour happened and was deemed worthy of positive recognition at that time; to remove the reward effectively wipes out the significance of that event. There may be a temptation, with a whole class system such as the collecting of marbles in a jar (Canter and Canter 1992), to take away marbles for the misbehaviour of individuals in an attempt to capitalise on both an individual's sense of responsibility to the group and peer group pressure motivated by the eventual reward on offer. Two questions arise; the first is whether it can be guaranteed that the individual feels any responsibility to the wider group. Indeed, the pupils whose behaviour often causes the greatest concern for teachers are those who seem unable or unwilling to predict the effects of their actions on other people. The second question relates to the issue of the peer group pressure that it is typically assumed will occur. The hope may be that peers will have a quiet word with the pupil along the lines of 'Hey, come on, you're making it bad for the rest of us.' We have to ask ourselves whether this is a realistic expectation. Kohn is sharply critical of systems that mean the misbehaviour of individuals can delay or prevent the class from accessing a whole class reward in an attempt to encourage peer group pressure, suggesting, 'This gambit is one of the most transparently manipulative strategies used by people in power. It calls forth a particularly noxious sort of peer pressure rather than encouraging genuine concern about the well-being of others' (Kohn 1999: 56).

At this point we should highlight one approach that represents an exception to the principle that rewards, once given, should not be taken away. Some primary readers may be working in schools that operate the Golden Time system put forward by Mosley and Sonnet (2005). They present Golden Time as part of a whole school approach so, if it appeals to you as a method to use in your own classroom, we would advise reading *Better Behaviour through Golden Time* (Mosley and Sonnet 2005) to ensure you understand how the surrounding elements are intended to work together. In summary, under this system all children start the week with the same number of minutes of Golden Time each. If they infringe one of the Golden Rules, a minute of Golden Time is deducted. At the end of the week, pupils are able to engage in one of usually a range of Golden Time activities on offer. Those who have lost minutes of Golden Time through the week have to wait for this period of time before they can join the Golden Time activity. For younger children, this system may be operated on a daily basis rather than over a week because they may not be able to make a connection between behaviour early in the week and the reduction of their Golden Time at the end. This system appeals to some teachers because it gets around the concern sometimes voiced that pupils who behave well most of the time do not get rewarded. However, this should not be interpreted as licence to do nothing else; Mosley and Sonnet (2005: 47) suggest 'we need to praise to the skies the child who keeps the Golden Rules all day, every term' and include some copiable Golden Time certificates in their book to support this. Under this system, the pupil who consistently behaves well gets a reward in the form of their full amount of Golden Time. Mosley and Sonnet (2005) suggest that it is important for those who have lost minutes of

Golden Time to be able to see the activity they would have engaged in if they had chosen to heed the warning given before the loss of minutes. The recommendation is to use a sand timer so that the waiting pupil can see the time passing. Mosley and Sonnet argue that this has an almost hypnotic quality and is preferable to a watch or clock that may be 'indecipherable to a child who is hot with emotion' (Mosley and Sonnet 2005: 44). If you are contemplating using this system, it is important to consider the management implications of potentially having several pupils waiting for differing amounts of time before starting their Golden Time activities. Some pupils will experience this as intended and compliantly reflect on the fact that had they made different choices they could now be engaging in the Golden Time activities others are enjoying. Others may experience and interpret the period of waiting differently and the reminder of what they are missing may fuel resentment and anger. Mosley and Sonnet (2005) provide some guidance on what to do with pupils whom they class as 'beyond' Golden Time, so again we would recommend you read their book if you are considering this approach.

Consistency between colleagues in the use of rewards

When starting in a new school, try to gain an understanding of how readily rewards are given by other teachers. This will enable you to gauge how frequently you should give rewards and what they should be given for. You may, of course, disagree with what you see and feel that pupils need rewarding more or less frequently. However, it is important to recognise that pupils will make interpretations of any deviation. For example, in a secondary school, if copious rewards are given in English but very few in Maths, this potentially raises questions for pupils in terms of whether the rewards relate in any meaningful way to their performance in these lessons or are just a reflection of individual teachers' personalities. In a primary school, if the pupils are used to receiving frequent rewards in Year 3 but move to Year 4 and find they do not get as many, it may raise the question for some of whether they personally have become worse in their learning or behaviour.

It is difficult to remove entirely the subjective element in the use of rewards, but schools and individual departments can benefit from scenario-based staff development activities that explore what the response would be in a particular situation. The key points to explore through such activities are:

- the methods used before formal rewards to acknowledge and reinforce academic and behavioural effort, improvement and achievement
- use of the school's formal rewards system to acknowledge and reinforce academic and behavioural effort, improvement and achievement.

Monitoring the distribution of rewards in your class

Activity 6.1 provides a snapshot of the use of positive feedback but it is probably not an exercise that it is feasible to repeat often. Nevertheless, it is important to informally self-monitor who you are directing positive comments towards and who receives primarily negative comments or possibly no comments at all. It is easy to fall into a pattern where it is the same pupils who receive the positive comments all the time and the same pupils who receive the negative or corrective comments. Inadvertently, a relationship is built between the teacher and pupils based on these interactions, and there is even a risk that the teacher may over-focus on those who misbehave and end up picking up on minor behaviours that from other pupils might not be noticed.

The distribution of formal rewards is easier to monitor. If some form of recording is not already built into the system, we would suggest that you find some means of keeping track of the pupils to whom you are giving rewards. It is important to monitor in relation to, for example, ethnicity, gender, special educational needs and disability, and to take appropriate action when distribution implies that there may be some bias (DCSF 2009a).

As we have previously suggested, rewards should indicate what is valued by accompanying them with positive feedback, but unless you monitor the distribution there is a risk that you inadvertently convey messages about *who* is valued.

Conclusion

Through our experience, we would suggest that schools and individual teachers are now better at positively acknowledging pupils' behaviour than when the Elton Report (DES 1989) made its comment that pupils could only get attention by working well or behaving badly. However, it would be rare to come across a teacher who praises or rewards pupils *too* much. As we have intimated within this chapter, the reason why there is still a degree of reticence may be the implication in the use of the word *praise* that this needs to be fulsome, glowing and possibly gushing. This naturally triggers thoughts about whether we should be expected to or need to praise pupils for complying with basic expectations. Praise within the behaviour for learning approach is reframed as positive feedback and should be viewed in terms of a form of encouragement focused on the learning behaviours exhibited. It is intended to protect and enhance the pupil's relationship with self, relationship with others and relationship with the curriculum by providing information on behavioural performance. It is for these reasons that we advocate that rewards are also accompanied by positive feedback.

There will be some pupils who seem unmoved by positive feedback and rewards or even actively reject them. This should not be surprising, given that individuals experience and interpret positive feedback *as individuals*. It is important to recognise that not all pupils find the same types of reward motivating and so it may be necessary to consider how a rewards system that broadly works for the majority needs to be adapted for individuals. This might require giving the positive feedback more privately or depersonalising it. The pupil themselves might be able to provide some information on what they would like to happen when they have done something well. Asking them should therefore be included as an option when trying to problem solve, if the usual combination of positive feedback and rewards appears to offer little appeal.

CHAPTER 4

MANAGING LEARNING IN CLASSROOMS

WHAT IS CONTROL FOR?

It might be helpful to clarify exactly what we are looking for in terms of the working atmosphere in the classroom. The statements of politicians in this area suggest that control *in itself* is 'a good thing' (see Figure 4.1 for some examples).

There is already a considerable amount of disaffection and disengagement from learning in British schools (Beadle, 2009; Elliott *et al.*, 2001; Elliott and Zamorski, 2002; Hackman, 2006; Ofsted, 2005b); the idea of turning schools into boot camps to improve things is a fanciful one. The complete elimination of disruption is not a realistic aim unless the 'rules of engagement' are changed in a way that goes substantially beyond what has been suggested in recent legislation.

Teachers' views on control were more instrumental, rather than regarding control as an end in itself. They wanted to have enough control to teach in whatever way they wanted, and for pupils to be able to learn without some spoiling the learning of

Figure 4.1 Politicians' statements about discipline in schools

'Children sitting quietly in lines of desks' (Party Leader, 'Old style discipline urged for schools', *Guardian*, 1 January 1994).

' "Oh my God, you'd have them all sitting quietly wouldn't you", "Well, what's wrong with that", I say.' (MP, *Westminster Education Forum*, 2006: 7).

'Secondary moderns can be excellent. I visited one where children stand up when an adult walks in.' (Party Spokesperson on Education, *Guardian*, 14 March 2006).

'We will not allow a single child to disrupt the education of children who want to learn.' (Party Leader, *Daily Telegraph*, 20 January 2000).

'The ethos of private schools … good discipline, high standards' (Education Minister, BBC News, 23 October 2005).

others. It should not be necessary to get pupils working silently in rows of desks in order to maintain control of the classroom; ideally, teachers can work in much more expansive and flexible ways and *still* be in control of proceedings. The word 'relaxed', however, occurred in many teachers' descriptions of what they wanted in terms of control in the classroom, as in this response:

> *Unless you are in control of your classes, you can't enjoy teaching. You want enough control to be able to relax, to feel that you can pretty much do what you want in terms of lesson format, and that you can get them quiet when you want, and they won't talk while you are talking.*
>
> (NQT)

> *Your teaching actually improves when you are at level 10 because you are at ease and you can think on your feet more clearly, you can come up with better ideas, better exposition and questioning because you've only got one track to think about, not two.*
>
> (Second year of teaching)

There were some interesting parallels here with pupils' views on the working atmosphere in the classroom. In what might appear a paradox, pupils expressed a dislike of teachers who were 'strict', but had a clear preference for teachers who were able to keep control of the classroom and stop pupils from spoiling the lesson (see Chapter 5 for further development of this point).

From the teachers' perspective, control is necessary so they can teach (and enjoy their teaching) and so pupils can learn, in whatever lesson format the teacher chooses.

HOW MUCH CONTROL DO YOU WANT?

If you want to be at point A on the scale below, you may have gone into the wrong profession (perhaps the armed services or the prison sector would be better?). There was a consensus among the teachers who were interviewed that it was no longer possible to physically frighten pupils into behaving well by using aggressive behaviour or by threats:

■ **Figure 4.2** How much control do you want?

A Palpable air of fear when you walk into the classroom.
B When the occasion demands, you can conjure up 'a whiff of fear'.
C You can get the class completely quiet and attentive by a simple word or gesture.
D Pupils will not talk while you are talking.
E You can get the class quiet with a bit of time and effort.
F The class is 'bubbly', a bit rowdy, and there is some muttering when you talk, but there is no real challenge to your authority.
G Some pupils will not always immediately do as they are instructed, you have to work hard to get basic compliance with instructions.
H Some pupils do not comply with your requests, you have to turn a blind eye to some things that are going on in order for the lesson to continue for pupils who might want to learn.

Certainly, shouting doesn't help at all. Kids aren't scared of teachers anymore. When I was at school we were scared of some of our teachers. Now they know that there's nothing you can do to physically intimidate them. You can't do it by anger, force, noise.

(Second year of teaching)

We don't have any sanctions that are available to us that would scare kids into compliance apart from perhaps reporting their behaviour to their parents in some cases.

(Assistant head)

They know their rights, they know that teachers are not allowed to hit them and aggressive, threatening behaviour is generally counter-productive.

(Year head)

For pupils not to talk while the teacher was talking (point D on the scale) was felt to be a key level to aspire to (point C was considered by many teachers to be desirable, but more difficult to achieve):

This is the biggie. Unless you can get them quiet, even if just for five minutes at the beginning to explain the task, your lesson is sunk, you can never really relax and feel that you have reasonable control of the lesson.

(Second year of teaching)

I regard it as a sort of litmus test as to whether things are satisfactory with a class or not. It's a key stage of getting a class to be as you want them in terms of their behaviour.

(NQT)

You need to be at level 9 or 10 to have a satisfactory question and answer interlude with pupils, and that is a very common form of lesson activity. If kids are talking through this, it's not going to work well, you're not really in control of things.

(Head of department)

Whole-class discussion is really hard when you start teaching. It takes time to establish your ground rules and procedures, and some trainees don't work patiently enough to get the pupils accustomed to these over a period of several lessons. But when you can have a relaxed and ordered, under-control discussion with a group, it really opens up a lot of possibilities.

(Teacher educator)

Another facet of 'control' that emerged as important to teachers was that they felt able to undertake a wide range of teaching approaches with a class, and were not limited by considerations of pupil behaviour. There was often an awareness that keeping control was being achieved at the expense of 'real' learning for pupils, but some saw this as a necessary compromise or 'lesser evil'.

I just know with one class that I would not take them out of the classroom into any public place because I don't feel confident that I would be fully in control of all members of the group. You know that this is not ideal, and that it is limiting the educational opportunities of some children, but you've got to be pragmatic, you can't risk having disasters.

(Second year of teaching)

You become aware that you start designing lessons around pupils' behaviour. I started giving them things to write down, get in their books. You don't like doing it because you know they're not learning anything, they're not doing anything worthwhile.

(NQT)

For instance, with some groups, I found that I couldn't turn round and write things on the board. If you turned your back on them for two minutes, they were off ... calling out to each other and messing around. So I stopped using the blackboard.

(Student teacher)

If you were walking round, from outside you might get the impression that perhaps as high a proportion as 70–80 per cent of classes were at levels 9 and 10, perhaps the average would be around 7, 8, 9 ... but inside the rooms you are sometimes aware that these levels are partly achieved by control strategies which limit how much worthwhile learning is going on ... teachers structure lessons so as to 'keep their heads down', and keep them busy. There are perhaps half a dozen teachers who will be struggling at around levels 3 and 4.

(Advanced skills teacher)

Teachers varied in their views about the level at which it was still possible to enjoy one's teaching, and the level at which they felt that the learning of pupils would be adversely affected by lack of control. Less-experienced teachers were more inclined to think that levels 6 and 7 on the ten-point scale (see Chapter 1) were 'okay' from both points of view. Experienced teachers tended to feel that lessons ought to be at levels 8–10 from the point of view of both teacher enjoyment and pupil learning, but there were exceptions:

I think I'm probably different to a lot of my colleagues, I've got very high tolerance levels, perhaps the highest of anyone in the school.... I have very noisy classes ... I think I could be at level 5 and perhaps still be able to enjoy it but I don't think I'm typical. But pupil learning, that's a different matter ... probably around level 7 or perhaps even above that.

(Advanced skills teacher)

Although there were variations in teachers' perceptions of the levels at which pupil learning and teacher job satisfaction were affected, it was possible to identify three important criteria about the degree of control which was felt to be desirable in the classroom (see Figure 4.3)

■ **Figure 4.3** Teachers' ideas about the degree of control desirable in the classroom

- The pupils will generally listen in silence when the teacher is talking.
- The teacher does not feel constrained in terms of what forms of classroom activity he/she can undertake because of class management considerations.
- The amount of learning that takes place in the lesson will not be limited because some pupils are impeding the learning of others.

Interview responses indicated that although the overall levels of challenge in the area of pupil behaviour varied significantly between schools, student teachers and NQTs would generally encounter many of the same problems whatever school they were working in in terms of day-to-day low-level disruption of lessons. The most commonly encountered difficulties are presented in Figure 4.4.

Although several recent enquiries have stressed that much of the disruption in schools is 'low level' and is of the sort described in Figure 4.4, it would be misleading to suggest that disruption is limited to such minor transgressions in all schools. There were several schools where more serious forms of disruption such as refusal, swearing and aggressive behaviour were not uncommon (see Chapter 8 for further development of this point), but the types of behaviour noted in Figure 4.4 were likely to be encountered by the majority of student teachers and NQTs. The list is not radically different from those emerging from other studies in this area over the past 20 years (see, for instance, Wragg, 1984; Elton, 1989; *The Teaching Student*, 1994).

Although new teachers will generally encounter similar forms of low-level disruption whichever school they are teaching at, the means of dealing successfully with such problems will differ. This is psychologically difficult for teachers in their early experiences of working in classrooms. For understandable reasons they are looking for 'a rule', a standard procedure, 'tell me what to do when X happens'. However attractive this might seem, it is not a realistic way forward, given the complexity of schools, classrooms and pupils. One NQT made this point in relation to the system of writing pupils' names up on the board:

> *At one of my teaching placement schools the kids would just laugh because they knew there was no system that would back it up at the end of the day, but here it works well in most cases.*

As noted in Chapter 2, the 'craft' knowledge of experienced teachers is rarely held in the form of universally applicable prescriptions, and most teachers are reluctant to stipulate a specific punishment for particular transgressions, although they are generally happy to suggest 'parameters' for appropriate action, and many of them believe in the patient application of pressure to get pupils into the habit of accepting and complying with particular 'ground rules' (see Figure 4.5).

Occasionally, there are gurus of class management who have sufficient confidence to advise specific courses of action and provide exemplar 'scripts' for particular classroom problems, but a glance at Figure 4.5 suggests that such prescriptive advice

▨ **Figure 4.4** The most commonly encountered problems of low-level disruption

- Not being quiet when the teacher is talking.
- Talking or 'messing about' with another pupil or pupils.
- Arriving late to the lesson.
- Not bringing equipment.
- Calling out/shouting across the room.
- Not getting down to work when asked to do so.
- Inappropriate/offensive remarks.
- Not completing homework.

■ **Figure 4.5** How helpful are prescribed courses of action?

Transgression	Action	What you should say to the pupil
Arrival late	Put pupil's name in a book. On subsequent occasions, parents should be contacted, and possibly the Education Welfare Officer.	'Everyone is allowed one late arrival. You've just had yours. See – your name is in the book.'
Cheek	The child has to be taken aside and told plainly that this behaviour is unacceptable.	'Get this straight. In no circumstances are you to be rude or to take the mickey out of adults. If you have a grievance, go to your form tutor. Report back here at 10:30 please.'
Comic behaviour	It is as well to make a pre-emptive strike as soon as misplaced humour rears its head.	'Tomkins, yes, you. Quite an amusing approach which we will discuss further at break. Meanwhile, back to our beloved decimals.'
Fidgeting	Much fidgeting arises from children playing idly, and with bad posture. Start the pen and ruler drill on day one and stick to it.	'Yes, you Shufflebottom. Pen in ledge, ruler behind it, exercise book closed. Now, both the ups – sit up and shut up.'

(Peach, 1988: 18–19)

may not be effective in all school contexts. There are classrooms where 'raising an eyebrow' or 'the look' may quell latent disruption, but there is obviously no 'formula' which is guaranteed to work in every instance.

As Beadle (2010) points out, given the enormous differences in the situations and personnel involved in these situations, it would be surprising if there was a form of words or specific teacher intervention that could guarantee a successful outcome to the interaction. Moreover, different teachers have different approaches to sorting out problems with pupil behaviour. It is often not a matter of the 'right or wrong' response, but how skilfully a particular strategy is implemented, and teachers playing to their different strengths and weaknesses. I once had a colleague whose approach was a very up-front and confrontational one. With a new class, he would go in and at the start of the first lesson, ask the class 'Who wants trouble?', making it clear by his intonation that if there were any pupils who wanted to attempt disruption, or to interfere with learning, he would address this immediately and make it an absolute priority to establish that all pupils in the class would accept his standards of classroom etiquette. I did not feel that this approach (certainly at that point in my career) was one which I could have successfully carried off. Similarly, in attempting to deal with the problem of pupils not bringing equipment, I was aware that my head of department, who was exceptionally accomplished at managing pupil behaviour, would not dream of simply lending pupils pens, pencils, etc. (the issue was a hypothetical one: none of Harry's pupils would dare to admit to arriving at his lesson without equipment). A kindly and perceptive senior teacher advised me that, given my standing with my classes at that time, it would be better to simply have a small supply of pens and pencils to lend to offenders, until my authority over the class was consolidated. It is not even simply a matter of degrees of authority, teachers have different styles and dispositions. Some see seating plans as a natural and obvious way of exercising control in the classroom, others prefer a more laissez faire or even 'democratic' way of running a classroom, and might only resort to moving pupils if they had forfeited the right to sit with their friends by betraying the teacher's trust (see the section on 'Moving pupils' for examples of teacher testimony about this). Figure 4.6 gives an indication of some of the different styles and dispositions that teachers espouse.

The next sections of the chapter address some of the areas many teachers found difficult in the early stages of their teaching, and explore some of the complexities of the principles of procedure which were sometimes suggested in these areas.

GETTING THE CLASS QUIET

This was one of the most commonly mentioned problems for trainee teachers in particular, and the most common piece of advice from mentors was not to talk over the class, and to wait for the class to be silent and attentive before starting to talk, as with a conductor about to start a piece of music with an orchestra.

Cowley (2002: 22) eloquently makes a case for the power of this approach:

> My first discussion with a new class is always about my requirement for silence whenever I address them. I make it clear that I will achieve this no matter what.... If you work with challenging children, or in a school where behaviour is a big issue, this is not easy. The temptation is to give up at the first hurdle, to talk over them in your desperation to get some work done. But consider the signals you are giving if you talk while they are not listening. The unspoken message is that ... you don't expect to be listened to.

▪ **Figure 4.6** Teaching styles, some continuums

Discursive or businesslike?	Some pupils like it when the teacher is willing to go off the subject and talk about 'other things', others find it indulgent and irritating. Some research evidence suggests that pupils prefer teachers who are purposeful and focused, where they learn nearly all the time; other research suggests that pupils like teachers where they can have 'a bit of fun' at least some of the time. Much depends of course on how much teachers go off-track, and how skilfully it is done.
Flexible or consistent?	Some teachers can be creatively flexible about how they handle incidents and might even change from lesson to lesson, and be idiosyncratic about using sanctions in a way that pupils like. Others make a virtue of trying to be absolutely consistent over time so that the pupils know absolutely where they stand.
Pedantic or casual?	Some teachers like to line pupils up in twos before they come into the room, and have them standing behind their desks, with strict rituals about the start and end of lessons – and yet they can somehow make it fun and the pupils enjoy the rituals. Others like to keep rules to a minimum, as long as they can start when they want to, they are not bothered if the pupils chat as they come in. Similarly with registers, some like silence during the register, others are much more relaxed about this.
Friendly or formal?	Some teachers just have a much more informal and friendly style than others. Some pupils like this, others don't like teachers to be too 'chummy'. This can vary between schools and across age ranges.

'Talking over the class' is a common criticism of student teachers in the early stages of their first teaching placement, and this strategy emerged as a very commonly suggested course of action by experienced teachers and is a strategy that I recommend to my students. However, there are some classrooms where it doesn't appear to work:

> *I really tried hard to make it work ... I got to 23 minutes on one occasion but then gave up ... I was getting nowhere ... the kids really weren't that bothered. With this group anyway, it just didn't work.*
>
> (Student teacher)

> *One experienced member of staff told me that he had waited 40 minutes for them to be quiet. I just don't think that a new teacher would have the confidence to do that and I'm not sure that after a few minutes it's even the right thing to do.*
>
> (Second year of teaching)

> *We do have some classes now where even established teachers struggle to get them quiet throughout the lesson. Sometimes we have to teach to the pupils who want to learn, and try and ignore the ones who are messing around. Often if you do ignore the low-level stuff ... if you don't take the bait, they will settle down and just slump or mutter to each other. I honestly feel that more learning gets done this way than if I were to try and get things perfect before starting. I know it's not ideal but it's my way of getting through the day with my worst classes.*
>
> (Experienced teacher)

Cowley (2002: 22) goes on to suggest a range of strategies for following up this aim, including waiting for them to be quiet: 'If you have the nerve, call your students' bluff by waiting for them to fall silent. If you are willing to hold out, eventually many classes will become quiet without any further input from you.'

This is perhaps a good example of a principle of procedure, to be tested to see if it works or not. One of the standard questions I asked in the interviews with teachers was how they tried to get their classes to be quiet in order to start the lesson. Many of them mentioned the strategy of not starting the lesson until they were quiet. In two cases, teachers reported that it didn't work (after waiting 23 and 40 minutes). In several other cases, teachers questioned whether the time and effort spent waiting could be justified in terms of the teaching time lost:

> *With my most difficult groups in afternoon periods I still sometimes end up teaching over some talking, I still haven't got the power to get them all quiet for any length of time and the lesson would be too stop–start ... I'd waste too much time.*
>
> (NQT)

One mentor suggested that student teachers, for understandable reasons, sometimes lacked the confidence to persevere with this strategy long enough for it to work:

> *I see some trainees give up just too soon ... they start when the class is still not really quiet and paying attention ... they are nearly there ... if they just said 'We still don't quite have silence ... Gary? Alan...?' Another minute and they could have had them just so but they just didn't quite have the confidence.*
>
> (Third year of teaching)

Several teachers reported that sticking doggedly to not talking until pupils were quiet did work for them, although in several cases this took a considerable amount of time to achieve:

> *More than anything, it was just stubbornness and perseverance. Until Christmas, I was continually pointing out that they mustn't talk while I am talking. We have a five-steps system ... five times when your name is on the board for transgressions and they have to go out. I had to constantly use that system, marking it on the board when kids talked out of turn. It didn't seem to be working and then after Christmas, it started to take effect ... it started to work.*
>
> (NQT in a challenging school)

> *I had one year 8 class, I just couldn't get them quiet. On occasions, the deputy head had to come in to get them to be quiet. After a term of flogging the same rule, lesson after lesson, it has started to work. Even kids coming back into the class from the behaviour unit fall in with it ... they do what the other kids have got used to doing. I'm not saying that they are quiet all the time, or that things are easy, but compared to the first term, it's a transformation.*
>
> (NQT)

> *With a new class I make a conscious effort in the first lesson, the first week, to spend a lot of time and effort very reasonably but firmly and clearly getting across a few key ground rules.... Only two or three, and the biggest one is not talking while I talk. I make it clear that if they talk over me, I will pick that up, that is not OK and there will be a smallish, reasonable sanction applied. The second anyone breaks it, I pick it up. If you can just get this accepted and applied so everyone knows the score from week one ... that it's the norm that you don't talk while I'm talking ... it makes it so much easier and at our place this is achievable with most of the classes if you work really hard at it. It won't work if you have a rules overload ... if there are ten of them [rules] to remember and apply ... you're chewing ... your coat's not off, no turning round, no tapping, if you are going on at them about everything, being mercilessly and gratingly negative ... it won't work. First things first. If you can get them to be quiet while you are talking, that is a really important move.*
>
> (Fourth year of teaching)

> *It's a series of small steps ... I'll wait for quiet. If some are still talking I'll raise my eyebrow and make eye contact, just to give them a signal. Some of them will cotton on and stop talking at that point. I'll thank the ones who are quiet, 'Thank you 7R for being so helpful'. I'll ask one who is still talking, by name, to please stop talking. If they don't stop, I'll point out to them that if they don't stop talking, they'll have to stay behind at the end to see me about it. They know that I will do something at the end of the lesson to inconvenience them in some way. I try and give them every chance to comply. It takes a few moments and a bit of patience but at my school, with most classes and most kids, it works, partly because they're used to this ritual, this way of doing things. I'm aware that it might not work everywhere, or if you didn't know the kids. It takes time to get your routines and rituals established.*
>
> (NQT)

> *There are a few lucky people with such natural presence and charisma that it only takes them one glare and the students are reduced to silence. Not being one of*

them, the only thing I've found that works is sheer persistence – stopping every time you're interrupted and making an example of a couple of people early in the year – phone calls to parents and detentions, etc.

(Second year of teaching)

With the year 9s it's harder, they haven't internalised it yet so I can't just glance or warn ... I have to stop, praise and thank the one's who are quiet, restate the rules ... send out a yellow caution card message – if it doesn't stop I will have to take some specified action to discourage them.

(Second year of teaching)

You make progress gradually and at different rates with different groups. You need to adjust how you handle things according to how good or bad things are. With some groups, I'm confident enough to stop the lesson if there is someone talking. Pick out a few kids and ask them to be quiet please, politely but confidently, firmly ... ask them by name.

(NQT)

Another teacher talked of the importance of not forcing pupils to be quiet when it wasn't necessary:

'Silence is precious – don't waste it.' A cheesy motto perhaps, but remembering this has really improved my classroom management. Some teachers ask students to line up outside the classroom in silence; I think this is misguided – it penalises the good kids who arrive early. It's also a waste of good silence; why should children be silent if there's nothing interesting to keep quiet for? I make a big fuss about the parts of the lesson where silence is needed – I say something like 'Now this is the part of the lesson where you are going to have to be quiet for five minutes while I explain what we are going to be doing.' This is particularly important with lower-ability groups and groups with lots of ADHD kids; they have half a chance of containing their talking if they know how long they have to hold out for. With really tricky groups, I even get one of them to time me – and to add on an extra two minutes when somebody talks.

(Third year of teaching)

One last piece of feedback in this area; a teaching assistant, giving his opinion of how often the strategy of waiting for quiet appeared to work:

What surprised me was how often it worked.... Over 90 per cent of the time ... sometimes more quickly than others ... but not every time.

What conclusions might be drawn from such testimony? That just waiting for pupils to be quiet doesn't always work? That sometimes it doesn't justify the time it wastes? That sometimes teachers don't persevere with it for long enough? That it has to be used in conjunction with other methods to make it work – for example, picking up on pupils who are reluctant to be quiet and punishing them? That the chances of success depend on the school you are working in?

Several teacher educators suggested that one of the differences between student teachers who develop towards excellence in this facet of teaching and those who make less progress is partly a question of 'open-mindedness'. Has reading the extracts above made any difference to your views of waiting for silence; will your practice be in any way different as a result of reading the extracts, or will you carry on pretty much as before?

MOVING PUPILS

Another issue which was prominent in discussions about managing classrooms was whether or not moving pupils within the classroom was a useful strategy for limiting interference with pupils' learning, and whether seating plans were a good idea for assisting the teacher's control of the lesson.

As with waiting for pupils to be quiet, there was no clear consensus of opinion over the effectiveness of moving pupils within the class. Even within the same school, it was felt to work better with some classes than others:

> With some classes it works really well ... brilliant, a really good safety valve. With others they will just shout across the room to each other, it won't make any difference.
>
> (NQT)

> In this school, moving kids generally works. They will generally comply. I've only had refusal to move once. But they don't always behave perfectly once moved ... often you have to take consequences a step further by sending them out or keeping them behind or putting them in a detention.
>
> (Third year of teaching)

> Sometimes it does work, and it's definitely one of the strategies that trainees should experiment with. Sometimes I would plan where pupils sat so I could have some pupils as 'barriers' between others who they might combust with, but it doesn't work all the time ... with some groups you will just get the pupils you have separated shouting at each other across the room rather than being able to just talk quietly to their mate in a less disruptive manner.
>
> (Teacher educator who had worked at a school 'in special measures')

At some schools, moving pupils was thought to be of limited value; perhaps a step that had to be gone through on the route to removing someone from the classroom altogether, but a gambit likely to provoke hostility, argument and possibly refusal:

> It's a hassle to do it ... you have to at least try it sometimes as one of the steps that might come before sending them out altogether, but our kids know their rights and can be quick to get stroppy. The problem is that they often protest against being asked to move and that stretches things out ... it can take up lesson time as you get dragged into persuading them ... threatening them.
>
> (NQT)

> Yes, it's one of the sensible stages you go through. It will sometimes stop a group of two or three from getting each other into trouble ... sometimes they can't stop themselves. Sometimes it works. Sometimes they complain and resist ... 'move someone else, it's not fair' etc.... and it escalates. You've got to be polite, patient and firm ... not make big deal out of it ... steer them towards a low-level choice

... give them a way out: choice A ... not big deal, choice B ... you get in bigger trouble ... think about it ... you know it makes sense. Try and keep it light-hearted and low-key but once you've asked them to move, do everything you can to get them to do it even if in the last resort you do have to take serious measures at a later stage for the refusal.

(Experienced teacher)

One answer to the problem of wrangles over which pupil should be moved was to move both pupils:

A common problem with moving kids is that the one you move says 'Not fair ... why me, why not him...', so I move both of them to separate corners of the room. It just speeds things up sometimes, cuts down the potential for bickering and dragging things out. Of course, sometimes you just get both of them complaining. The main thing is that you don't want to get in a protracted argument that stops the lesson from continuing so you've got to sort it quickly whatever you do. You don't want an eight-minute stand-off with other kids observing with interest and some kids who would quite like to get on with learning getting cheesed off. So if you get refusal to move, give them a quick option, this or something more serious ... consequences, and if they keep it up, impose the detention or whatever it is.

(Experienced teacher)

One tentative hypothesis that might be advanced is that moving pupils would be more likely to work in an unproblematic way in schools with very strong systems for managing pupil behaviour and strong 'consequences' for pupils who might go beyond being moved to being ejected from the room, or who might get in much more trouble for not complying with the request to move immediately (see Chapter 6). The teacher responses chimed with Rogers' (1990) advice about ignoring 'secondary behaviour' (in this case, the moans and whinges about having to move), as long as the primary goal of separating two troublesome individuals was met. The biggest danger appeared to be that if the negotiations over the move were protracted, learning for the whole class would be put on hold, and all the other pupils in the class would have nothing to do other than observe the show, get on with their work quietly or decide to mess about themselves. There is sometimes a tension between sorting out a problem and maintaining the learning momentum of the lesson. Also, in some cases, insisting on a move led to escalation in the form of refusal to move.

Different tensions arose in the area of seating plans. Several teachers spoke positively of the use of seating plans:

It made a massive difference at the start of my second year. It sent a message ... you are not in the playground now ... it's not the messing about chatting to your mates zone, it's the learning zone, we are here to learn and I'm responsible for making this happen on behalf of the group.

(Third year of teaching)

At our place, I've found that seating plans work really well. It's nearly always worked ... I'm always amazed at how much better it makes things and wonder why I didn't try it before.

(NQT)

142

Prevention is better than cure – it's all in the seating plan. If a kid is sitting next to two people that he doesn't like enough to talk to, but doesn't hate enough to wind up, the most interesting thing around should be your lesson.

(Second year of teaching)

However, this was felt to be a strategy that was much easier for established teachers to use, from the start of the year. It was felt to be much harder for student teachers who were coming into the class at some point during the year, when it was likely to lead to 'we were here first' resentment, or for NQTs who decided to move towards the use of seating plans half way through the year. In the words of two respondents:

It's always best when you start straightaway with it rather than bringing it in later, then they can get resentful about it rather than just accepting it.

(NQT)

Seating plans from day one – much easier than bringing it in later as a response to problems.

(Experienced teacher)

There is also the issue of how the seating plan is presented to pupils. Brighouse (2001) makes the case for 'non-provocative' ways of initiating seating plans, planned to coincide with new learning experiences rather than being explicitly imposed to assert control.

Some teachers felt uncomfortable about seating plans for other reasons, which related more to what sort of teacher they wanted to be. As noted earlier in this chapter, there are some continuums in terms of teaching 'style', and one of them is between being controlling and relaxed in approach. The following extracts are examples of teachers explaining why they didn't use seating plans:

Teachers have different styles and you've got to choose the one you're comfortable with. I usually let them sit in friendship groups and then move them if they mess around … I let them move back with their mates next lesson, I don't keep them apart…. Sometimes being easy going and relaxed works as long as you do take action appropriately if they do start to go too far…. Our kids respond well to this on the whole.

(Experienced teacher)

I feel uncomfortable making them sit to a plan. It feels mean and punitive, as if it assumes the worst of pupils, it sends negative messages. Perhaps it's more efficient in a horrible sort of Victorian way but a lot of pupils have little enough fun in school and being able to sit next to your friends as long as you behave doesn't seem a lot to ask. I prefer to have a default position that you can sit where you want as long as you don't mess about.

(Experienced teacher)

Pupils' views on seating plans were unequivocally negative (see Chapter 5): one of the biggest causes of resentment against school and against being in classrooms was not being able to sit with friends.

There is a possible tension here between classrooms as 'democratic spaces', which respect pupil friendships and autonomy, and teachers exercising 'leadership' in the classroom 'for the pupils' own good', and so that they will find it easier to control the lessons. As in so many areas, there is a judgement call to be made here by new teachers, which will depend on school culture (to what extent are pupils used to being told where to sit?), the custom and practice of the preceding teacher in the subject, the personality and educational philosophy of the teacher concerned, the nature of the individual class and the time of year when the seating plan is imposed. Suggestions for consideration here are that new teachers contemplating imposing a seating plan might ask for advice from teachers who have been *in situ*, and that they might at some point explore both methods of working and see which works best for them.

SENDING PUPILS OUT

One of the most common dilemmas facing the teachers interviewed (and this applied not just to student teachers and NQTs), was what to do when they were not able to prevent one or more pupils from spoiling the working atmosphere in the classroom. In some cases the behaviour involved was extreme (see Chapter 7), and in a sense this made decision-making easier, but more often there were difficult decisions to be made about whether a pupil had forfeited the right to stay in the classroom. These decisions were complicated by the fact that schools (and sometimes departments) had different policies for dealing with such difficulties, different 'tolerance levels' for pupil disruption. The nature of the class and the 'pupil culture' within the school (see Chapter 6) can also influence the effectiveness of taking such action against pupils. In some schools, a group of pupils may tacitly or overtly support the pupil who is being sent out. In other circumstances, pupils may well be on the side of the teacher doing the sending out:

> We are lucky here because generally the kids are glad to get rid of them ... 'Nice one, he's out of the room', I can tell that they are pleased about it, that you've sorted it out, done something.
>
> (NQT)

This was not the only example of other pupils' attitudes influencing decision-making about whether to send pupils out. In the following instance, the fact that other pupils were 'onside', and not colluding with a difficult pupil led to a teacher deciding *not* to send the pupil out:

> I couldn't claim that his behaviour had no effect on the quality of the lesson for the other pupils ... but the lesson kept going, the pupils learned something, it wasn't perfect but nearly all the pupils were 'onside', they could see that I was doing my best, trying to be reasonable. They were tacitly on my side even if they couldn't do much to help.
>
> (Four years in teaching, working in a difficult school)

Although to some extent it was often down to the individual teacher's judgement as to whether and in what circumstances to send pupils out, decision-making was influenced by school and departmental policy and practice. In some schools, there was an understanding that if a pupil could not be prevented from interfering with the learning of others, even at quite a low level, they should not be allowed to stay in the classroom. In others, teachers were encouraged to regard sending out as a last resort, and even then, to try to get pupils back into the classroom as quickly as possible, after a few minutes 'cooling off' time and a warning about their behaviour.

In some cases, teachers' decisions were influenced by how efficiently school systems worked:

> We're not supposed to put kids out in the corridor. The system is to send them to the 'Remove' room if they are misbehaving to the extent that they are spoiling the learning of others. Someone is supposed to come and get them and take them down. This sounds great but it can take 20 minutes for someone to arrive, and in the meantime you've got to just put up with the kid spoiling your lesson. Sometimes there's no one there or no one comes because whoever is on the Remove room is off or has forgotten. It's made me realise that I just have to get on with it myself. Perhaps it's good because it's made me really think hard about what I can do, how to react, it's made me more self-reliant, but I am jealous of fellow NQTs who've really got a close support network of people in the department.
>
> (NQT)

One NQT talked wistfully of being on placement at a school where two burly non-teaching staff came at almost instant notice and led troublemakers away to an exclusion room, but this level of service did not appear to be widely available.

It would be helpful for new teachers if there was a clear set of criteria for when to send pupils out, such as the principle outlined by one head of department:

> If they are disrupting the learning of others ... stopping pupils who would like to learn from doing so, and they don't stop after requests and warnings ... they should go out.

However, while this might be eminently practicable in some schools, in others it was not felt to be feasible:

> There was a timeout room but it was for extreme behaviour ... less extreme things you were supposed to just send them out for a few minutes to calm down, have a quiet word with them just outside so they weren't acting up in front of their friends. Everybody knew that if you sent out every kid who was messing about, the system would be overwhelmed. It was not ideal but you just had to manage things as best you could, in terms of damage limitation. What is the best I can do here given that the situation is dire?
>
> (Second in department in a school in special measures)

These examples underline the importance of teachers having to be flexible, resilient and self-reliant. Part of learning to teach is about how to handle things when the situation is *not* perfect. Given the range of people and factors influencing the quality of life of the trainee or NQT, it would be surprising if all colleagues and all facets of a school were perfect. Several experienced mentors suggested that a degree of 'adaptability', 'quickness to adjust, pick things up' was a helpful quality for new teachers as opposed to those who were 'waiting for the answer lady to come round' (teacher educator). In the words of another teacher educator:

> *It's about their intelligence in ascertaining what the boundaries of acceptable 'normal' behaviour are. It's not just about your values and standards, but the school's, and these vary enormously. In some schools they run a very tight ship and you are expected to send kids out if there is the slightest interference with learning, in others you are expected to cope with quite a lot and keep them in (the classroom). It's the speed with which some trainees tune in to the norms and conventions which operate in particular school contexts. It's about how quick they are to pick things up, to learn and adapt.*

In addition to 'health and safety' issues, and violent, aggressive or threatening behaviour, one of the criteria that was mentioned by many experienced teachers for sending out was persistent and 'targeted' disruption, in the sense of behaviour that had the deliberate intention of wrecking the lesson:

> *If it's calculated ... if they are quite deliberately trying to sabotage the whole lesson and it's a sustained attack designed to stop learning taking place. Then you have to send them out.... You can put up with some incidents if it's spontaneous – some of our pupils are very volatile but they are just children, they do have emotions, some of them are genuinely very troubled and they do get upset sometimes. We're the adults, we should be able to understand that and if it's just a moment of silliness or lack of control and then they stop and settle down, that's usually okay.*
>
> (Fourth year of teaching in a difficult school)

> *Is it a one-off incident where you can say 'never mind, see me at the end about it', or a sustained attack on the lesson, a deliberate challenge to your authority which is going to carry on until you do something about it? If it is the latter, you do perhaps move to thinking about getting them out of the lesson if you have tried warning, moving and so on.*
>
> (Experienced head of department)

> *We have some kids here who find normal classroom behaviour very difficult. They do not have self-discipline, self-control, basic manners. But that is just how they are, they are not cynically trying to spoil your lesson in a premeditated way. You have to try and finesse them into being okay, settling them down, learning to get on with them, cajoling them into getting on with the work. Skilful handling can keep kids in the classroom. Some teachers kick out a lot more than others. Sometimes it's the right thing to do to send a kid out, but you can't just send dozens of kids out on a regular basis. Some corridors are almost like a refugee community during lessons because so many pupils have been sent out.*
>
> (Head of year in a difficult school)

> *Sometimes it is necessary, it's the right thing to do, not a sign of failure on your part, but unless it's a major atrocity which is ongoing, just for a few minutes, to calm things down, have a quiet word and try and get them back in and settled.*
>
> (Head of department in a difficult school)

146

It's like raising your voice, you get diminishing returns if you do it too much ... plus if you've already sent one kid out, it doesn't work as well, they're beginning to get strength in numbers – they've got a friend to play with, talk to, discuss how to wind you up some more ... you're building up a little insurgency out there.

(Teacher educator)

Almost without exception, the teachers and heads interviewed felt that there were times when sending pupils out was an appropriate course of action; as a safety valve, to allow for 'cooling off', to assert the teacher's right to teach and to protect the rights of pupils who wanted to learn.

Experienced teachers also had views about *how* to send pupils out. A commonly expressed view was that some student teachers and NQTs were too indecisive, 'dithered', warned but did not then act, and often left it too long to send pupils out:

I had to be on the ball in terms of being clear about picking up the first one to go too far after a clear warning, then a particular person could be dealt with by the department, and the others would quieten down. If you don't pick things up early, and leave it until a few of them have gone beyond what's acceptable, it's much harder because you don't know where to start, it's too widespread, you are being arbitrary and unfair, you've lost it. I've learned to act earlier and more decisively, I don't let it get out of control before taking action.

(NQT)

I've become more decisive about sending pupils out, I'm more clear in my own mind about when it's necessary, when it's the right thing to do. You tend to be a bit uncertain in your PGCE year. Give them a clear warning or warnings and then go ahead and do it and don't wait too long.

(NQT)

What kids hate is when there's a lack of consistency, when punishments are arbitrary, when 'it's not fair' and other pupils can see it's not fair.

(Head teacher)

Some are too timid to intervene. I sometimes ask, 'Why didn't you send him out of the classroom?' And they say, 'Because you were here'. They see it as losing face, a sign of weakness. They let things slide until lots of kids are messing about and then panic and send someone out without a warning, just pick on someone at random because they have become flustered under pressure.

(Teacher educator)

The majority of respondents advocated a 'low-key', understated tone and manner for asking pupils to go out of the room, rather than angry and declamatory words and gestures:

Don't do it as if it's a big deal ... 'Just wait outside for a minute and I'll come out in a minute when I've just set this task....' When they are out, mention the options ... go back in, just get on with things quietly ... that's it, all over, forgotten ... just get on with it quietly.

(Head of department in a difficult school)

I try and do it in a low-key way, not showdown at the OK Corral ... 'Can you just wait outside for a minute and I'll pop out and have a word with you in a minute.' Perhaps open the door and then carry on giving some instructions to the rest of the class. And then quietly go up to them if they haven't already gone out and remind them that they've got to go out, I haven't forgotten.

(Third year of teaching)

Another common problem with sending out pupils is that they often seek attention from outside the room; jumping up and down outside the window, pulling faces, tapping on the window, asking if they can come back in yet. 'Tactical ignoring' was the most commonly recommended response to this:

Just send them out for 5 or 10 minutes, so they get bored and want to come back in. And if they are messing about outside, just ignore them, get on with teaching the class, they generally just subside after a few minutes and slump quietly.

(NQT)

Some trainees send them out for too long, forget they are out there and then kids go wandering off. You've got to keep a bit of an eye out if you send them out, but not let them know that. Try and be relaxed and calm with the rest of the class and then pop out nonchalantly to have a word with them.

(Head of department)

Whether sending out pupils 'works', whether pupils behave when they are allowed back in, whether they agree to go out or refuse depends on what further steps are available to the teacher, the 'tightness' of the school system for following things up, the degree to which the teacher is prepared to follow up incidents of disruption, and the extent to which parents will be supportive of the school. One interesting question is what happens to a pupil who has had to be sent out of a lesson and then continues to misbehave? Nothing? 'Is that it?', or will 'consequences' follow? And who will take the time and trouble to sort out the consequences? The teacher who has sent the pupil out or 'the system'? Head teachers and heads of department both suggested that the teacher who had done the sending out should try to take at least some responsibility for following things up:

Sending pupils out is a possible next step, if moving them within the classroom hasn't worked. Ideally, in a good school or departmental system, there will also be the option of further steps, like sending them to the time-out room, or to sit in someone else's classroom. If bad behaviour is repeated in the next lesson, and the one after, something more serious needs to be done, and this may involve parents, year head and so on. But teachers need to be prepared to put time and effort into following things up, keeping kids in, contacting parents and so on. They shouldn't just pass it on to someone else. It's what happens after the lesson that usually determines whether pupils' behaviour is sorted out.

(Teacher educator)

When you talk to them outside the class, when they are not in front of their friends, explain to them that this is getting serious, it is significant. They can either come back in and keep their head down until the end of the lesson, and that will be the

> *end of it, or there will be serious consequences and their behaviour will be the subject of more serious deliberation ... this could be form teacher, year head, contacting parents. Explain the options to them clearly.*
>
> (Head of department)

What refinements might teachers consider making to their practice in the light of these comments? This might depend on the nature of their current practice in this area. They may already tend to send pupils out too precipitately if anything, so the suggestion that some teachers wait too long before sending pupils out does not apply to them. But teachers can reflect on how their practice compares to that of other teachers within the same school, and whether they make any of the misjudgements mentioned above. They can experiment to see if adjustments to their usual way of doing things makes a difference, and they can ask other teachers (especially those whose levels on the ten-point scale tend to be high) how they handle the issue of sending pupils out.

REFUSAL

Sending pupils out was acknowledged to be one of the teacher actions (together with asking pupils to move within the classroom) which might lead to pupil refusal to comply with a teacher's request. The prevalence of pupil refusal obviously varies from school to school. In some schools it rarely occurred, in others it was 'very common'. There was a

■ **Figure 4.7** Sending pupils out: 'It's what happens *after* the lesson that usually determines whether pupils' behaviour is sorted out'

general consensus among teachers that refusal should be taken very seriously, and was not something that could be just forgotten about or glossed over:

> *Something must happen to send a message to all the pupils that this is not acceptable. Ideally, it would be that the child is sent home until the parents come in to discuss the matter, or the child is taken out of circulation for a period so that other pupils understand the seriousness of refusal. There is a safety issue here. Who would want to send their kids to a school where the kids routinely don't do as the teachers say?*
>
> (Experienced teacher)

> *Refusal is one of the few things I call for help on; it is suicide to let a class see somebody refusing and getting away with it.*
>
> (Second year of teaching)

> *You can't run a school where the kids can pick and choose whether they do what the teacher says. It's important that something happens if a pupil refuses, that it is seen as very serious and unacceptable. Even if the sanction doesn't 'cure' the problem, doesn't deter the pupil from refusing again at some point, it must be clear to the others that there will be serious consequences if they do not do as the teacher tells them.*
>
> (Head of department)

One teacher used refusal to take off coats at the start of the lesson (a school policy), to remove uncooperative pupils from the lesson at an early stage:

> *At the beginning of every lesson, I insist that children take their coats off and put MP3 players away. Some teachers don't bother with this at my school, but for me it's the litmus test of a child's willingness to accept my authority. The chances are that if they won't take their coat off, they won't do anything else I ask either. The coat test gives me the excuse I need (after the requisite three warnings) to send any complete refusers to the withdrawal room.*
>
> (Second year of teaching)

Although there was a consensus that refusal was very serious, and that some form of serious 'consequences' should unfailingly apply to pupils who refused, teachers did not feel that it was politic to 'use such force as is reasonable' (DfEE, 1998b: 4) to remove the pupils from the room, especially in the case of a trainee or NQT.

The act allows teachers to 'use such force as is reasonable' if a pupil is committing a criminal offence, injuring themselves or others or causing damage to property. More pertinent to teachers' day-to-day lives, the act also sanctions teachers to use reasonable force if pupils are 'engaging in any behaviour prejudicial to maintaining good order and discipline at the school or among any of its pupils, whether that behaviour occurs in a classroom during a teaching session or elsewhere' (DfEE, 1998b: 4).

Almost without exception, teachers felt that 'reasonable force' should only be used against pupils in extreme situations, such as if a pupil was endangering the health and safety of others. They did not feel that force should be used in the case of pupil refusal, and generally felt that teachers should always try and keep 'an appropriate professional distance' between themselves and pupils. Simply reminding the pupil of the seriousness of refusal and trying to point them towards less serious courses of behaviour, and then sending a pupil for a senior member of staff or following the refusal up later if the pupil remained obdurate, were more commonly suggested ways forward:

> *Certainly I would never march or frogmarch or drag them out of the classroom ... that seems to me a recipe for escalation. Even if you attempt to 'guide' or steer them out, you are in dodgy territory. Regulations might talk about 'reasonable force' but it is a grey area ... who is going to decide what's reasonable ... what if some other kids' description of what you did or views on what is reasonable differ from yours ... what if there is no other adult in the room as a witness?*
>
> (Second year of teaching)

> *At our school, the protocol on this is clear; you always try to get another adult present in such circumstances unless there is an urgent safety issue.*
>
> (Mentor)

> *In this school, refusal is very common. When they have had their warnings, they come to the last one and often refuse to go out. You are then in the hands of the school system. I've learned that you can often deal with it later. If they don't go out, that's their problem, they know that they will be in trouble later because of this and I notice that they often go quiet because they know that they will be in trouble and they have gone too far. I used to spend a lot of time and emotional energy trying to get them to go out, now I just get on with the lesson and move on. There's no 'show' for them all to enjoy, you try and just get on with the learning, not let them have the show they are looking for.*
>
> (NQT in a difficult school)

> *They don't always go out quietly, sometimes they do refuse ... and I'm one of the senior team who go round the school picking kids up and sorting out things like this ... taking them down to the remove room. One kid in my lesson last week just point blank refused to leave the room. So I just said he'd have to do a half-hour detention and moved on. It wasn't a prefect solution but it allowed me to move on to something else ... to carry on with the lesson – but you have to make sure that you follow it up – the kid does the detention.*
>
> (Head of sixth form)

Even in difficult schools, physical restraint issues were felt to be unusual situations, not day-to-day occurrences, but there was a clear view that using force to control pupils was an absolute last resort:

> *In our school, there is very little need for physical contact and restraint issues ... I've been in classrooms now for two years some of which was spent in difficult schools and it's never happened ... it's never come to that.*
>
> (Second year of teaching)

> *Physical contact? Do it as little as possible, but the dictum during my training to not touch the children at all isn't realistic. You do sometimes have to break up fights and I have been advised that the next time I do it, I should say to the child 'I am holding your arms because you are putting your safety and the safety of others at risk.' Last time I broke up a fight one of the parents complained, but the HOY*

151

gave her short shrift; I'd expect most schools would support you as long as it was clearly necessary to touch the child.

(Second year of teaching)

In the PGCE year or when I started here I would not have gone near a pupil, not have even thought of it. Now I am established, it's less of an issue, not a big deal but I'm still careful. I might just touch the back of someone's bag and point them in the right direction or signpost them to move in a particular direction, hold my arm out to shepherd them somewhere ... relaxed and low-key. It's a judgement issue that comes with knowing the kids you are working with and being comfortable with them.

(Second year of teaching)

Avoid it at all costs ... no, at almost all costs. With all rules there's always an exception. Don't give people a rule and say it's unbreakable. The world of teaching is too complex for that but.... It should be absolutely a last resort, there's usually a way round it. Unless, there's a safety issue ... if a pupil is endangering the safety and well-being of other pupils.

(Teacher educator)

I have done it [been in physical contact with pupils] and have usually regretted it afterwards. It's about being professional, and once you get into that territory, it jeopardises that. You take it into territory where they are more at home than you are, into their world. You need always to be in control of yourself. Once you are in physical contact with pupils of one sort or another, you are in dangerous and unpredictable waters. Having said that, if pupil safety is involved, you have to step in.

(Teacher educator)

HOW DO TEACHERS COPE WHEN THEY ARE NOT IN FULL CONTROL OF THE CLASSROOM?

Both the interview responses and the questionnaire surveys (Haydn, 2002) suggested that many teachers have to teach classes where they do not feel in completely relaxed and assured control and are not working at levels 9 and 10 of the ten-point scale (see Chapter 1). Many teachers acknowledged that they sometimes had groups where they did not enjoy their teaching. How did teachers respond to that situation? A variety of suggestions emerged (see Figure 4.8).

Some of the coping strategies were as much philosophical as practical. One strand of this was remembering that (usually), lots of teachers are finding it difficult to get to level 10:

I'd had a bad day and my mentor advised me to just have a walk round the school during a lesson when I wasn't teaching. I saw other teachers having a tough time and it made me feel a lot better.

(Student teacher)

We do have issues with behaviour. We've got some lovely, lovely kids, but also a small minority who are really difficult. I've had to develop a thicker skin, to realise

Figure 4.8 Coping strategies

Change the format of the lesson	*'I change the order of things. Do my "fun" starters at the end of the lesson instead of the beginning as a reward for being cooperative … being reasonable.'* (NQT) *'With the worst groups I've stopped "classic" teaching in the sense of having some sort of exposition, oral introduction to the lesson. I don't talk at the start. When they come in, the activity will be on their desks and I will tell them to do it straightaway. Even with really tough groups, some of them will just get on with it, or will slump, heads down. This narrows down the number of kids you have to sort out. Then you work on them, by name, trying to cajole them, settle them down. And I try to have something planned as a reward for the end of the lesson … we'll finish with a video if …'* (NQT) *'I used to resort to a series of worksheets, do-able tasks, fill in the missing words, things to keep them occupied. Now I'm more experienced I would probably do it differently, but then that was the only way I could get through the day.'* (Seven years in teaching) *'If it's Thursday or Friday period 6, I have to make radical changes to my planning. There's a real difference in terms of what I can do with them and my planning has to take account of that. You just develop a better understanding of what school is like from their point of view. A lot of them have had enough, they don't want to be in your lesson they want to go home, they are looking forward to messing about with their friends and socialising. You've got to bust a gut to make it either really structured and purposeful, or try really hard to have something that might interest them, grab their attention, at least try and plan a bit of fun or interest into the lesson, even if that means going a bit all over the place in terms of content.'* (NQT) (Several teachers mentioned using short extracts of a 'watchable' video as a means of getting through the lesson with difficult groups).
'Keep going'	*'I've learned that you have to take some things with a pinch of salt. With some groups you have to let some things go, just pick up on big things.'* (NQT in tough school) *'With some groups I just plough on, just keep going unless there is a major atrocity. Sometimes they subside a bit when they realise that I'm not rising to it, that I'm just carrying on with the lesson, and they just put their heads down, slump over the desk. I know the theory is that they get worse and worse until they find out what your limit is but this doesn't seem the norm.'* (NQT in tough school)

153

'Keep calm'

'I still ignore some things, you can't pick everything up, but this one thing – not talking when you're talking – that's a key one. But if you start "Where's your tie boy?", "Put that gum in the bin now", "You, stop banging that ruler", "Stop swinging on your chair", "Turn round now" … it's about priorities, the art of the possible, one step at a time.' (Third year of teaching)

'I learned to battle through. You have to let some things go … sometimes even some of the ground rules you've been trying to establish … because it's one of those days and you just do the best you can. You've got to keep going, don't stop, focus on the kids who are learning and complying even if there are not many of them.' (Mentor)

'It is important not to start getting narky with all of them just because you are under pressure. You've got to stay polite, calm and reasonable, even if you don't feel like that inside. You need the patience of a saint some days and you've got to be fairly thick-skinned … you mustn't take it personally.' (NQT)

'The biggest thing was just learning to keep calm under pressure. Don't let them wind you up. I learned it almost by accident when I went in one morning feeling really tired and not very well. I didn't give up, I didn't just let them do whatever, but I perhaps came across as a bit more relaxed and they didn't seem up for it as much.' (Second year of teaching)

'I know you're not supposed to do it but I would sometimes pop out for a minute … not far and with an excuse … but it sometimes just gave me a chance to compose myself, to calm down, to gather my resources for another round.' (Third year of teaching in a tough school)

'I remember the Bill Rogers thing about dealing with the things you can control, not the things that you can't control. I try really hard to keep calm, even when provoked, I try hard not to let it get to me. You can make a mental effort not to get angry or upset or exasperated and that has helped me.' (NQT in a tough school)

154

that it's not just me, it's not personal. You see other, more experienced teachers having trouble and it makes you feel better.

(NQT at a school 'with serious weaknesses')

You worry about it and if you are sensible, you talk about the issues, the pupils who are doing particular things to give you a hard time, and this usually helps to get things in proportion. It might not provide a magic answer but you realise that it's not that big a deal, it's not beyond the parameters of what's happening to other teachers.

(Teacher educator)

One advanced skills teacher talked of how important it was to try to not take it personally when pupils were aggressive and rude, and how difficult it was to do this:

It is incredibly hard not to take it personally, not to think that their awful behaviour should in some way have been prevented or minimised by you. I still take it personally after all these years, even as I tell younger teachers that they mustn't take it personally. It is crucial for your psychological well-being at this school but that doesn't make it easy to do.

'Keeping things in proportion' was also suggested as a strategy for coping with unsatisfactory pupil behaviour and deficits on the ten-point scale. Remembering that level 10 is not a natural state of affairs, and that lots of pupils with problems are prone to misbehaving and 'trying it on'. In going into the world of classrooms, you are in a sense leaving the adult world with its developed and generally accepted conventions of appropriate behaviour and going into an environment where many of the inhabitants have not yet understood and internalised these conventions, and part of the teacher's job is to help them to get there:

It's not a nice feeling not being fully in control of a lesson but you've got to keep things in perspective. Not giving up, not stopping trying but being philosophical about things not being perfect. Not thinking that life will never be the same because 8R were not fully under your control.

(Teacher educator)

Some of them [teachers] seemed to have the ability to shrug things off ... to think after a bad lesson, a rough ride ... tomorrow's another day, to learn to be resilient. Not to give up, to stop trying, but not to just brood about it in a sort of negative, passive way.

(Teaching assistant)

Some teachers were just so professional ... always calm, polite and composed, even when they were under pressure. Some of them also seemed able to put incidents behind them once they were over ... to walk away from it and just move on to the next class.

(Teaching assistant)

It might be helpful to think in terms of a sort of 'Richter scale' of pupil atrocity to try and keep things in perspective:

> *I think of the atrocities that happen in the world … 9/11, beheadings, terrorism, muggings – or even the stuff that happens in this school, and in the great scale of things the fact that one small child with problems doesn't want to do the work doesn't seem such a big deal. I've still got to try and do my best to sort out the best possible way forward but it doesn't seem quite so desperate.*
>
> (NQT working in a difficult school)

TEACHERS' VIEWS OF THE CHARACTERISTICS OF COLLEAGUES WHO WERE GOOD AT MANAGING LEARNING IN THE CLASSROOM

Pupil behaviour and classroom climate are influenced by factors other than teachers' 'organisational' skills in managing learning within the classroom. Much depends on the planning that has gone into the lesson (see Chapter 3), on the skill with which teachers interact with pupils (Chapter 5) and teachers' assiduousness in following up incidents after the lesson. However, teachers did have opinions about the 'within-class' skills that were likely to be conducive to good pupil behaviour. The six most frequently referred to qualities are described below.

1 Getting started with the learning: not letting anything stop the learning

The DfES (2004: 7.3) has pointed out that learning 'can often be derailed by administrative and organisational tasks' (a degree of irony here). One mentor spoke despairingly of a trainee who would often spend several minutes giving the books out, or spelling out rules, dealing with administrative matters, clearing up missing homework, talking to pupils who arrived late. Experienced teachers had a range of strategies for dealing with pupils who were late, or who arrived without equipment, but the underlying principle behind action was to not let these matters take up a second more learning time than was essential: to get them started on learning as quickly as possible and sort out possible reprisals later, perhaps at the end of the lesson. It was felt that some student teachers and NQTs allowed pupils to 'stop the learning', and drift into a situation where the teacher was 'telling off' someone, but where there was nothing much for the other pupils to do, so that they too drifted into 'messing about'. One teacher suggested that it would be an interesting experiment for teachers to time how long it took them to get all the pupils in a class either listening and attentive, or working.

> *We give them something the second they come in. You've got to try and get the learning going as soon as possible, to get them engaged and interested. Don't give them time to think about messing about because they are bored and nothing is happening. So sometimes we are waiting at the door as they come in and give out a post-it note or sheet or something that they have to do. Or something on the board which they can all get going with.*
>
> (Advanced skills teacher)

> *I try to set a purposeful tone to the lesson from the moment the kids walk in. When the students come in, the starter is already up on the board, so the majority*

156

of students settle down straight away and get on with it; then I can concentrate on picking off any naughties – people who won't sit down, don't have a pen, refuse to take their coat off, etc., and I try to get this done as briskly as I possibly can.

(Second year of teaching)

The kids can tell straightaway ... that some teachers mean business. The control comes from the first few seconds of the lesson, right from the start, the way they come into the room. With some teachers, within a few seconds of them coming into the room, the pupils are learning, the lesson has started. With others, ten minutes have gone by and there is no learning going on, the lesson hasn't really started, it's still chaos, lots of kids aren't sure what they are sup-posed to be doing and some ... an increasing number, are starting to mess around ... there are some pupils who in spite of all this are quiet and well behaved, who are just resigned to the fact that here is yet another lesson where some kids will spoil the lesson, where it will all go pear-shaped, where they will not get to learn ... they quietly and philosophically just watch or doodle in their exercise books.

(Teaching assistant)

Rogers (2002) points out that getting the pupils prepared for learning can start even before the start of the lesson by 'corridor calming', to remind pupils of the transition from 'social time' to 'learning community' time, and several experienced teachers described how they met pupils as they came into the room, just to settle things down.

2 Clear instructions

Fontana (1994) argues that this is an aspect of managing learning in classrooms that is undervalued. In the pupil survey (see Chapter 5), many pupils' main complaint about being in classrooms was that they simply did not understand what was going on and what they were supposed to be doing. Many of the teachers interviewed also regarded instruction as an underrated skill, and one which was perhaps 'taken for granted' by some student teachers, who might assume that pupils would be as quick to take things on board as adults:

The teachers who are good at this are calm, purposeful, organised, know what they are doing. If it gets a bit chaotic, they are prepared. Instructions are very clear. The pupils know exactly what they are supposed to do ... they cannot plau-sibly say that they don't know what to do because it is so clear. When pupils are not sure what it is they have to do, that's when things start to get iffy.

(Teaching assistant)

On first placement, a lot of trainees are not clear in giving instructions to pupils about the tasks to be done, and don't realise the need to patiently repeat those instructions so that the pupils know what they are being asked to do. It's a real art, giving really clear instructions and patiently, calmly reinforcing them.

(Teacher educator)

One teacher had the idea of 'The Core', meaning the absolute minimum that pupils needed to do, clearly spelled out:

I ask myself, 'Do they know what the core is ... the absolute minimum that they have got to do if they are to leave the lesson without consequences?' I have the list for the core on the board so I can point to it at any time in the lesson. The core must be absolutely manageable for any pupil. So that there is no excuse for not doing it if it gets referred upwards ... they will not have a leg to stand on if they have to explain it to a deputy or year head. 'You must do at least 15 lines...' and I will point to the line that they have got to get to avoid consequences.

(Third year in teaching)

Cowley (2003) also makes the point that repetition and modelling are vitally important tools for controlling pupil behaviour. Sometimes there is no substitute for showing pupils what you want them to do, going through it with them, giving them the first example, worked through. And pupils often do need to be told what to do more than once; they won't all get it first time round.

3 'Clear warning, then do what you said you would do'

Several teachers used the metaphor of 'the yellow caution card' to stress the importance of giving pupils a clear warning before imposing a sanction. Having given a clear signal that if a pupil does not desist, the teacher will do something reasonable, plausible and specific, it was felt to be important that teachers should be as consistent as possible in doing what they said they would do. Vagueness, 'bluster' and false last chances ('I won't tell you again', repeated several times) were not thought to be helpful. I can remember walking past a class in the school where I used to teach to hear a teacher saying to the class, 'If you throw one more thing at me..', and being met by a volley of missiles (mainly paper) reminiscent of the battle scene in the Olivier version of Henry V. More words were spoken but no action was taken. Decisiveness, polite and calm firmness, consistency and being 'eminently reasonable' were mentioned as desirable characteristics:

A punishment should never come as a surprise to a pupil. It should be apparent to them and to everyone in the room that it is coming. They shouldn't be able to say, 'Well, that came out of the blue, I'd no idea the teacher was going to do that.'

(Teacher educator)

It quickly becomes apparent to pupils whether or not a teacher is actually going to do something if they mess about ... whether there will be any consequences. Pupils quickly work it out ... 'he's not actually going to do anything ... he's just going to keep telling us off' ... then some of them start exploring exactly how far they can go ... because that's what some kids are like.

(Teacher educator)

If teachers just keep telling them off ... nagging them, continually sending out negative signals, betraying exasperation and impotence ... or jumping up and down, getting narky, speaking in a loud 'teacher' voice ... it's actually worse than doing nothing. Just ignoring it and getting on with the lesson, trying to work round the fact that some kids aren't behaving well would be better ... not ideal but at least it wouldn't make things worse.

(Teacher educator)

A couple of weeks ago I was doing a roleplay and they were messing around so I stopped it and went back to working from the textbooks. After that ... after I had done what I said I would do ... they would stop when I threatened to stop a 'fun' activity. They realised that if I said I was going to do something, I would do it.

(NQT)

The kids actually said to me ... 'Go on sir, you keep saying you are going to kick X out if he farts again but you just warn him again and again. You never do it do you?' I felt I couldn't be seen to then respond to that but it made me realise that I had just been going on about it without doing anything. This was obvious to the whole class. You would think this would be obvious, that you would know you were doing it, but I didn't.

(NQT)

If I learned one thing from the lecture on class management it was to follow things up between the end of one lesson and the start of the next.... If a pupil has been going out of their way to mess you around and give you trouble, do whatever you can to show that you can inconvenience them, and that you have a lot of resources at your disposal ... taking breaks and dinner times, the school system, form and year teachers, heads of department. And when this works it makes you feel more confident about sorting out other pupils, other classes.

(NQT)

The worst of all worlds is to consistently rebuke the whole class as a body, without singling out individuals who have behaved badly, and to not take any action against those individuals but continue with group denigration. Brophy and Evertson (1976) argue that this creates a 'negative ripple effect' with classes, and leads even the more compliant pupils to siding with disruptive elements.

4 'Calibration' and choice

Teachers spoke of the skill with which some colleagues carefully 'graded' their responses to pupil transgressions, and went through a series of carefully considered steps, of gradually increasing seriousness, from the most polite and friendly of requests, to calmly but firmly sending a pupil out of the room. They did not 'close-off' options by using a high-level sanction too precipitately, thus leaving themselves less room for manoeuvre later, and leaving a smaller range of intelligent 'choices' for pupils:

It is possible to intelligently anticipate the sorts of thing that might occur and to make contingency plans ... at least think through what your options are in terms of steps ... friendly, polite but firm request to stop doing whatever it is ... clear warning of minor, low-level, eminently reasonable consequences if they don't comply, a sort of yellow caution card ... whether there might be a stage where you invoke the school system or colleagues in the department, form teacher ... year head. Some trainees are better than others at this sort of anticipation and contingency planning. Some go from nothing to thermo-nuclear in one step.

(Teacher educator)

You've got to point them towards the right choice. . . . 'Do A and you will get in less trouble than if you do B . . . you won't be inconvenienced . . . you won't get hassled as much . . . think about it . . . is it worth it?'

(Three years in teaching)

They like group work so you can offer that as a reward if they do a written task or behave reasonably during QUAD work. You can use the textbooks as a warning. If you are OK . . . group work, if not . . .

(NQT)

Olsen and Cooper (2001) make the point that it is important to have a clear hierarchy of sanctions in dealing with pupil transgressions, and to deploy them consistently over time. Vacillation, indecisiveness and inconsistency can antagonise pupils further. One teacher made the point that with some teachers, pupils have got a pretty good idea of what will happen to them when they do something wrong before the teacher has said anything about it.

5 Looking at the pupils and noticing what they are doing, how they are feeling

This again perhaps sounds like stating the obvious, but several mentors felt that some student teachers were more alert and aware to what was going on in the classroom than others, and better at 'reading signals' from the class – about whether they had stopped listening, had switched off, were getting restless or needed a change of activity, an attribute Wragg (1984) termed 'withitness', and that might be regarded as a combination of observation, alertness and sensitivity (see Chapter 7 for further explanation and development of 'withitness').

6 Perseverance

Together with being 'quick to learn', perseverance was the quality that was mentioned most frequently by teachers to explain why some students and NQTs became more successful than others in managing their classrooms:

As much as anything it's about persistence and consistency. It took a while with some classes but now things don't usually go below around level 7. It's about developing a shared understanding of the parameters of what's acceptable.

(NQT)

I teach in what some might call a 'bog-standard' comprehensive school . . . we get some kids who are just a delight to teach and some who can be quite difficult but who you can get through to if you work hard at it and do the right things consistently.

(NQT)

I did have to battle with some classes when I came here . . . with kids who had been here at this school before me . . . who are you, new person, who do you

160

think you are? A bit of it is about determination and perseverance. Not giving up. You are not going to win, we will have a good lesson. It's a sort of sense of will that eventually gets through to them. You gradually get more of them on your side.

(NQT)

Obviously they [student teachers] are going to have to work with some classes that are difficult ... that are tricky even for experienced teachers. The test here is whether they are resilient, whether they keep trying in the face of consistent failure and disappointment over a series of several lessons rather than being passive, not trying anything, not even asking about what they might do. They are not judged on what levels they get to, they are judged on whether things are going in the right direction and whether they kept trying.

(Head of department)

I spent most weekends of my NQT year obsessing about a year 8 class that tortured me every Friday period five and every Monday period one. I was annoyed with myself at the time for letting them ruin my weekends, but the hours I spent reading and planning and thinking about how to deal with the little beggars paid off in the end. I teach the same class this year and most of them have chosen History for GCSE.

(Second year of teaching)

Several mentors and heads of department felt it was helpful to survival in the classroom if the trainee or NQT could differentiate between the things that they could do something about, and the factors that were beyond their control. It was a question of finding the right point on the continuum between giving up because the situation is hopeless, 'these kids are impossible to teach', 'this school is a zoo', and pointless and counter-productive self-flagellation because you can't make things perfect. Teachers have to be pragmatists. It's about having a sophisticated understanding and good judgement of 'the art of the possible': asking the question, 'what is the best I can do for this group of pupils given the circumstances, and the factors which are beyond my ability to change?' and answering it intelligently. This is illustrated in the following extracts, from an experienced and successful head of department, working in a challenging school:

It's the art of the possible ... sometimes there isn't an easy answer. It's a matter of damage limitation. Your job is to do the best you can in the circumstances ... to battle away and get as many pupils as possible to learn in spite of everything. It's partly about determination to keep going ... to get across to them that we are here to learn, that learning is important.

(Four years teaching in a tough school)

Teacher testimony suggests that with some teaching groups, it takes time, patience and perhaps an element of remorselessness to get to the higher levels on the ten-point scale. No 'quick fixes' or easy solutions were apparent. There was certainly an element of 'training' or behaviourism in establishing basic ground rules for behaviour and an ethos of 'we are here to learn' in the classroom. But they also spoke of massive benefits in return for the hard work invested in this endeavour, in terms of the quality of teachers' working lives, the degree to which they could relax and enjoy their teaching.

■ **Figure 4.9** 'What helped you to get better at managing pupil behaviour?'

 A survey of 75 PGCE students two-thirds of the way through their course of training asked them to identify what they had learned about managing pupil behaviour from their own experience, from observing experienced teachers and from advice from experienced teachers. The outcomes of the survey can be accessed at: http://escalate.ac.uk/5618 (pages 153–9).

(Haydn, 2009c)

Many were also keen to stress that once ground rules and patterns of working have become established, and relationships with pupils put on a stable basis of mutual respect, life gets a lot easier, and less time and effort is required in terms of how much following up and 'sorting out' of pupils is required. Pupils sometimes become 'unthinkingly quiet' when the teacher talks or wants to start work, because they have just got used to the teacher's way of doing things, and it is this 'unthinking' good behaviour that is perhaps one of the hallmarks of really getting to level 10 with a class.

It's important to remember, it's not a battle. It's a campaign, in that the result is decided over a period of time, a series of lessons, not within one lesson or a few days. And it's a strange sort of campaign, in that the struggle is partly to persuade 'the enemy' that you are really on the same side (see Chapter 5).

SUMMARY

■ It can be helpful to think about what control is for and how much control you need in order to be in relaxed and assured control of the classroom.

■ Decision-making in this area is often about finding the right point on a range of continuums rather than 'right or wrong' judgements.

■ There are commonly encountered problems related to pupil behaviour where teachers need to experiment with a range of approaches to see what works best in particular contexts.

■ Teachers often have to make hard decisions about whether to keep difficult pupils in the classroom or to send them out of the class, and these decisions are, to some extent, influenced by school 'norms' and cultures.

■ There are sometimes occasions where there is nothing you can do to get a pupil or pupils to behave perfectly within the course of the lesson, and you have to think about what to do when you are not in complete control of the lesson.

■ Experienced teachers have a view about the characteristics of colleagues who are accomplished at managing pupil behaviour.

■ Making significant progress in improving the working atmosphere in class-rooms with particular teaching groups was generally thought to be a gradual and sustained process rather than something that could be achieved within the space of one or two lessons.

For Product Safety Concerns and Information please contact our
EU representative GPSR@taylorandfrancis.com Taylor & Francis
Verlag GmbH, Kaufingerstraße 24, 80331 München, Germany